DESIGNING INTERACTIVE SOFTWARE

Greg Kearsley
&
Robin Halley

Park Row Press
La Jolla, California

Kearsley, Greg, 1951-
Designing interactive software.

Bibliography: p.
Includes index.
1. Interactive computer systems. 2. Computer software--Development. I. Halley, Robin, 1944-
II. Title.
QA76.9.I58K431985 005.1'2 85-28463

This book was composed by the authors using an Apple® Macintosh™ and LaserWriter™.

First printing, 1985, Release 1.0
Second printing, 1986, Release 2.0

Printed in the United States of America.

ISBN 0-935749-25-X

Preface

Every day, more and more people are using computers in their daily lives. This has resulted in a tremendous need for well designed programs. Many different types of people are now involved in the development of software and need to know how to develop good programs.

Creating quality software is easy if you follow a relatively small number of design rules. This book will introduce you to the principles underlying the design of interactive programs. It covers screen design, user control, response processing, helps, troubleshooting, and quality review. The nature of interactivity, the development process, and software support are also discussed.

Although this book will be useful to any software developer, it is primarily written for the person who is creating computer programs for the first time. It will also be useful to any programmer who lacks specific experience designing interactive software.

The guidelines provided in this book apply across all types of applications, all types of computers, and all types of programming languages and systems. This is true because the guidelines are based upon the way people learn and think. Regardless of the type of application or computer involved, the rules for designing good software are the same.

This is a style guide not a *how-to* book. It does not tell you the steps to follow in order to create good interactive programs. It tells you what principles to follow and what to avoid. Programming techniques are not covered since there are many other books available that describe good programming methodology. References to these books are provided in an Appendix.

We would like to thank Wendy Ebersberger for her editorial work on this book.

San Diego, CA.
April 1986

Contents

- Part I: Background -

Contents

- Part II: Guidelines -

Contents

Contents

PART I:

BACKGROUND

1/ Introduction

There are many *thick* books available on the design and development of software. This book is a style guide intended to provide a concise summary of the most important guidelines for designing interactive programs. If you follow the principles outlined in this *thin* book when designing software, you will consistently create good quality programs. Of course, you may need to read some of those *thick* books to learn how to do this.

About The Book

The book is divided into two parts. Part I provides some useful background to the guidelines presented in Part II. You do not need to read the chapters in Part I if you want to put the guidelines to immediate use.

Part I consists of four chapters. This first chapter addresses some important issues in the design of interactive software. These issues include:

- elements of software quality
- common software flaws
- hardware considerations
- programming languages/systems

Chapter 2 discusses the nature of interactivity and provides some examples of interactive sequences. The examples include a sign-on, multiple choice question, simulation, intelligent advisor and spreadsheet sequences.

Chapter 3 provides an overview of the development process including requirements, specifications, prototyping, and pilot testing. It also discusses different approaches to development and development time/costs.

Chapter 4 covers software support. This includes the design and use of reference manuals, user guides, training materials, job aids, and telephone hotlines.

Part II consists of six chapters that provide guidelines for the design of displays, user control, response analysis, error handling, helps, and quality review. Each chapter presents a set of general rules that apply most of the time. However, these rules are not to be followed dogmatically. Good design often requires "breaking the rules." Becoming a good designer involves knowing when to stick to the rules and when to deviate.

A few words about computer terms and concepts. This book does not assume any previous acquaintance with computers. However, a certain amount of computer terminology is necessary (e.g., bugs, variables, windows). In order to keep things concise, these terms are used without explanation but are defined in the glossary. So, if you run across a word you don't understand, please take a few seconds to look it up in the back of the book.

Elements of Software Quality

One of the critical skills needed by a software designer is the ability to distinquish a good program from a bad one. Actually, evaluation skills and design skills are mirror images of each other. If you know the elements that result in a well designed program then you also know the criteria to use in evaluating the quality of programs. In this section, we will briefly discuss the elements of software quality.

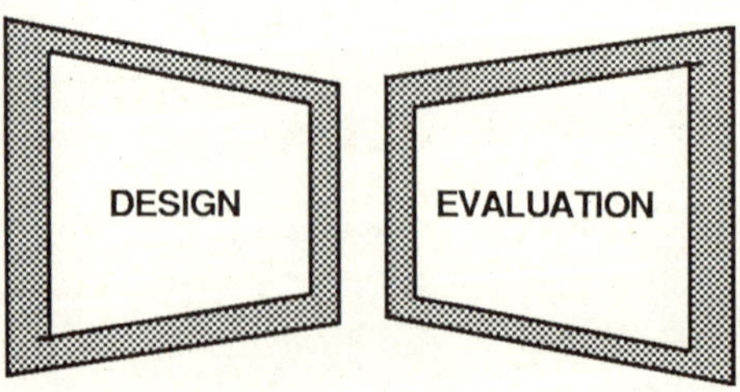

Software design and evaluation are complementary activities.

Table 1-1 lists some major characteristics of good interactive software. A program is valid if it is accurate, complete and current. For example, an accounting program with mistakes in its formulas or a billing program that displays mismatched customer records would not be valid!

Table 1-1

Characteristics of Good Interactive Software
VALID - Content is accurate/complete/current
USABLE - Minimal learning time and errors
MOTIVATING - User is interested/involved
VISUALLY STIMULATING - Captures attention
FLEXIBLE - User in control
RELIABLE - Consistent and free of bugs
USEFUL - Something is accomplished

Usability is measured in terms of the amount of time required to learn how to use a program and the number of mistakes or errors made. A program that has high usability will take very little time to learn and result in few user errors.

Motivation is an important characteristic for some types of programs. If a program is interesting and enjoyable, there is a greater chance it will be used.

Because computers are primarily a visual medium, it is desirable that screen displays be stimulating and well organized. Effective displays capture attention and facilitate performance. In some applications (e.g., radar displays, medical monitoring systems, process control displays), the easy understanding of screen displays is of critical importance.

To allow users to tailor a program to their needs and interests, it is important that the program offer a lot of flexibility over pace and sequencing. It is imperative that the user have ample control of the program.

A program must be very reliable in order to be trusted and believed. This means that the program must be consistent in the way it works and be free of bugs.

Finally, a program must be perceived as useful by users, i.e., they must feel that they have accomplished something by using it. Many programs are not perceived as useful because they do not do exactly what the user wants.

It is important to note that quality is incremental in nature rather than all or none. One program is better than another because it includes more aspects of good design. In other words, good design means paying attention to lots of different things. There is no single feature or characteristic that produces "quality". Each element makes a contribution. Of course, some features are more significant or noticeable than others.

Software Flaws

Another way of looking at software quality is to examine the typical problems reported by users. Many people describe their experiences with computers as frustrating, confusing, and unpleasant. Table 1-2 lists some of the most common problems.

Table 1-2

Typical Problems With Software
RIGID - Too much precision required
INCONSISTENT - Program is unpredictable
DENSE - Too much information at one time
JARGON - Terminology is obscure
NO FEEDBACK - Responses not acknowledged
FRAGILE - Poor error handling and recovery

Programs that allow no variability in response format, do not allow errors to be corrected, or will not allow information to be changed are perceived as too rigid by users. Even though programs may require very precise input, it is not a good idea to expect the user to respond precisely.

1/ Introduction

Inconsistency is a frequent source of user frustration. Input may be required in one format in one place but another format somewhere else. Function keys may have different actions in different parts of a program. Inconsistency translates into a perception of unpredictability by the user.

Displays or response sequences often contain too much information for a user to process easily. It is relatively easy to design programs that are so complex, they overload most users. Human performance limitations (particularly immediate memory capacity) need to be taken into account in program design.

Jargon is a perpetual problem in the computer world. There is a tendency to carry over computer terminology to the design of commands, error messages, directions, etc. The use of jargon often makes simple things very complicated for users.

Failure to acknowledge user responses or provide feedback that explains what the program is doing/has done, often leads to confusion. If people are going to trust a program, they must understand what it is doing. Providing feedback also helps users keep track of where they are in a program. Getting "lost" while using a program is a common user complaint.

Programs that are very fragile (i.e., break easily) are another source of annoyance to users. Poor error handling typically causes this problem. This problem can also be a consequence of other flaws already mentioned, such as the program being too rigid or dense.

The kind of problems just discussed all result from the failure to follow the design principles outlined in Part II of this book. Poor quality software fails to observe these rules.

Appendix A provides an evaluation checklist that can be used to assess the quality of a program in terms of the design principles discussed in Part II. The checklist allows you to compare programs quantitatively. This checklist will also help you identify specific design flaws in a program.

Hardware Considerations

This book does not deal with any specific brand of computer, nor does that matter much from a design viewpoint. The guidelines provided herein apply to any type of machine in the same way that good construction techniques apply to any type of building or proper engineering methods apply to any type of bridge. If you know how to design good quality software for one brand of computer, you will be able to do it for any machine or system.

What does make a difference are the specific features or capabilities of the computer you want to design for. For example, if the computer has a color graphics display, then you are going to be interested in design principles for color and graphics. Similarly, if it features touch input or speech output, you will be interested in the design aspects of these features. Table 1-3 summarizes some of the machine features that are likely to have design implications.

Table 1-3

Machine Features With Design Implications

Color	How many colors?
Resolution	How much detail can be displayed?
Graphics	What kind of illustrations are possible?
Cursor Control	How precisely can things be located?
Function Keys	How many are available?
Video Output	Will video/audiodisc be used?
Memory (RAM)	How much space is available?
Speech I/O	How many words/What quality?
Multi-user	What can/will be shared?

One of the difficult problems that you are likely to encounter is that the machine or system you are designing for has different *configurations*. On many personal computers, the user decides whether to have a monochrome or color display. Similarly, networked systems may have many kinds of terminals or personal computers attached. To the extent that you are designing programs for a machine or system that only comes in one configuration, your job is much easier.

For example, with the Apple® Macintosh™, all machines have the same built-in graphics display, a mouse, and a standard software interface incorporating icons and pop-up menus. On the other hand, with an IBM type of personal computer, users are likely to have different monitors, input devices, operating systems, and memory configurations.

What do you do as a designer when you don't know what options and capabilities a user will have on their computer? You have three logical choices:

Choice 1 - Design for the minimum configuration of the machine (e.g., monochrome display, minimum memory).

Choice 2 - Design for a machine with a specific set of features (e.g., color graphics with a certain amount of memory) and make it clear to the user that your program requires this configuration.

Choice 3 - Design for multiple configurations of a machine. In other words, design your program so that it can be used with a monochrome or color display, with or without touch input, etc.

Clearly, which of these alternatives you choose depends upon the context of your development effort. If you are developing a program for internal use in your organization, you may know the characteristics of the machines it will be used on. In this case, choice 2 or 3 is possible. If you were developing a program for commercial sale, you might opt for choice 1 or 3, since you want the program to run on as many machines as possible.

While choice 3 is the most general solution, it is also the most expensive since in most cases you will need to create somewhat different programs for different configurations. On the other hand, choice 1 is the safest and least expensive solution but one that does not take full advantage of the features that are possible with the machine. Choice 2 is also safe in the sense that you are going to specify exactly features the user's machine must have.

Actually, things are somewhat more complicated than we have

discussed so far. In addition to the hardware features listed in Table 1-3, the particular system software in use can also make a difference. For example, with the standard DOS operating system, a personal computer is not capable of graphics capabilities such as icons, pop-up menus, and overlapping windows. However, with a system manager such as Windows (Microsoft), GEM (Digital Research) or Topview (IBM), these kind of capabilities are possible. So, in addition to worrying about different hardware configurations, you also have to take system software into account.

To summarize this discussion about machine dependencies, the particular brand or type of computer does not matter from a design point of view. However, the possible configurations of the machine you design programs for may have important implications.

Programming Languages

This book does not deal with any specific programming language that might be used to create an interactive program. From a design point of view, it does not matter what programming language or system is used. Just as a writer does not normally know or care how a book is typeset, printed and bound, you don't need to know or care how a program you have created is programmed, debugged, tested and duplicated.

Of course, you may be curious about the implementation process and you may want to learn how to do it yourself. In that case, you will need to deal with a specific programming language. However, the programming step is beyond the scope of this book. Appendix B provides some recommended readings about programming style.

It is commonly believed that the selection of a particular programming language makes the difference between a good and bad program. This is false. The design of good quality software is a function of design experience, a good understanding of the application involved, creative talent, and, of course, knowledge of design principles for interactive programs. It is not a function of the particular language or system used to create the program.

The language or system does make a difference in terms of how hard or easy it will be to implement a certain design. While virtually any language or system can be used to create any program, in some cases it is so time consuming or cumbersome, that it is not practical to do so. For example, a design may call for graphics that require a long time to create using the graphics capabilities of a certain programming language/system. In this case, it is possible to do the graphics but would take more time and effort than is reasonable or affordable.

In some cases, things specified in the design may not be possible with certain languages or systems. For example, many languages and systems do not provide the capability to display different type sizes or fonts. Some languages do not allow you to create complex graphics (i.e., illustrations) or animation, use a full range of color/shading, produce certain sound effects, accept pointing responses, etc. In this situation, it is necessary to alter the design (or select a different programming tool).

It is important to realize that the amount of time it takes to program something is not only a consequence of the specific capabilities of the software, but also a function of the programmer's skill and experience. A very experienced programmer can accomplish things that would take a less experienced programmer much longer to do (or could not be done at all). In many cases, the experience level of the programmer is much more significant than the particular language used.

To summarize, the design of a program is separate from its implementation. However, it is important to select a programming language or system that will allow your design to be programmed as you have specified. Similarly, it is desirable to select a programmer who has sufficient experience to complete your design in the most expedient manner possible.

Programming Systems

It is possible to create programs without actually programming by using a programming system (also called program generator). A common example is a screen building system that lets you create input screens as you want them and automatically generates the corresponding program. Many database management programs allow you to specify the formats of the input screens and output reports; this is a form of program generator.

There are three domains where programming systems are fairly well developed: graphics, instruction, and expert systems. It is possible to create just about any type of graphic presentation desired from simple charts to complex manufacturing diagrams with commercially available graphics systems. Similarly, it is possible to create a wide range of instructional programs using authoring systems. Expert system generators allow you to produce an expert system program without any explicit programming. Some examples of these systems are described in Appendix C.

Programming systems have a number of advantages. They let you create software without having to know how to program. They speed up the development process since a lot of the detailed work is done automatically by the system. Most importantly, programming systems generate bug-free programs and therefore save debugging time.

It seems very likely that more and more programming systems will appear in the next few years, eliminating the need to use a programming language for most applications. While programming systems do substantially improve the efficiency of program development (chiefly by reducing the time required for debugging), they are still highly dependent on the quality of the design effort. For example, a screen builder will make it easy to create a display once you have decided how you want it designed. If you lack knowledge of good screen design principles, the screen builder will help you build terrible screens very efficiently!

Summary

The basic elements of software quality are validity, usability, motivation, visual stimulation, flexibility, reliability, and usefulness. Quality is incremental in nature: the more elements present in a program, the better the quality.

Poorly designed programs are rigid, fragile, inconsistent, dense, full of jargon, and lack adequate feedback. They are perceived by users as confusing, frustrating and unpleasant.

In general, the same design principles apply across all types of computers. However, different machines permit different kinds of design features (e.g., color, display resolution, input modes). A major consideration is that the same machine may have different options in terms of display, memory, or input/output devices.

A variety of programming languages and systems are available for creating interactive software. The particular language or system used to develop programs can have substantial impact on the development time required. However, the characteristics of the design itself are more important than the specific programming software used as far as quality and effectiveness is concerned.

1/ Introduction

2/ Interactivity

Almost all programs developed today are interactive to some degree (exceptions are certain sales demos, process control programs, and utilities). Any program that requires user input is by definition, an interactive program.

In this chapter, the nature of interactivity will be examined in detail. We will look at levels of response, types of interaction, and ways of representing interactive sequences.

Response Levels

The kind of interactivity possible can be analyzed in terms of the type of user response involved. Table 2-1 lists a series of different levels of response in order of increasing sophistication and associated response processing.

Table 2-1

Levels of Response	Response Processing Required
1. Single Key Press / Pointing	Match Key / Position
2. Multiple Choice Selection	Match Characters / Positions
3. Words, Phrases, Numbers	Keywords, Calculation
4. Multiple Responses	Match Sequence
5. Natural Language / Speech	Parser, Pattern Recognition

The simplest kind of response is a key press that indicates acknowledgement. For example, the user presses the space bar or the ENTER/RETURN key to see the next screen or data entry field. The next level of response is a choice from a list of options in a menu or a multiple choice question. The user chooses a particular response by typing a single letter or number, or by moving the cursor to that response. A more complex type of response is a word, phrase, or numerical answer that is typed in. A response that involves a sequence of responses that must be selected or typed in, represents a more complex response. The most complex type of response is natural language or speech input.

Clearly, the amount of information expressed in a response increases across levels. Compare the information in a single key press versus a natural language answer. The complexity of the response processing required also varies with the level of the response as shown on the right side of Table 2-1.

Key presses or pointing responses require only single character or positional matches. Reponses consisting of words, phrases or numeric answers require a series of string matches and introduce problems having to do with misspelling, order, upper/lower case, blank spaces, decimal places, etc. Multiple responses add the complexity of checking for sequence or position. Responses that are expressed in natural language or speech require parsers and pattern recognizers that employ artificial intelligence techniques.

To summarize, interactivity can be defined in terms of the level of response that a program requires. As the level of response increases in complexity, the complexity of the response processing needed increases correspondingly. The more complex the response processing, the more lengthy and involved the design process. In other words, the more interactive the program, the longer it takes to develop.

Types of Interactive Sequences

A second way of analyzing interactivity is in terms of different types of interactive sequences that can be used in programs. This represents a more global analysis of interactivity than looking at the specific types of responses in a program. Table 2-2 lists these sequences in order of increasing design complexity.

Table 2-2

Types of Interactive Sequences
Multiple Choice Questions
Simple Helps
Data Entry/Retrieval
Applications Programs
Simulations / Games
Process Control
Context Dependent Helps
Intelligent Tutors / Advisors

Multiple choice questions or options constitute the simplest type of interactive sequence. This involves the presentation of a question or menu option followed by a request for a response. Simple helps (i.e., fixed format) consist of a series of presentations and responses. Data entry or retrieval programs prompt for input or search keywords and acknowledge the input. Retrieval programs must format the output as well.

Applications programs such as word processing, database managers or spreadsheets involve unique response sequences associated with the problem the user is trying to solve using the program. The responses generated in a simulation or game depend upon the previous or successive values specified by the user for parameters or moves.

Process control programs depend not only on operator responses but also upon input from sensors. The outputs from process control programs often activate equipment as well as affect screen displays.

The advice provided by a context-sensitive help depends upon the current state of the task and exactly what the user is trying to do. Intelligent tutors and advisors build a model of the user to determine how to respond and handle user responses.

Each of these types of sequences represents an increasingly more sophisticated type of interactivity. The interaction increases in terms of uniqueness of input and user involvement. The questions or options provided in a menu, and the feedback provided, are not unique to a specific user. This is also true of data entry programs. However, the queries posed in a database search or the sequence of events produced in a game or simulation are likely to be one of a kind. Interaction in a process control program is also likely to be unique for each manufacturing run. The interaction created in an intelligent tutor is highly personalized and resembles a conversation between two people.

Increased interactivity also produces a higher degree of user involvement while using the program. Consider the degree of involvement that exists in a good video game or a realistic simulation. The user's concentration is very intense and all external distractions are blocked out. The response rate is very high and system response time is very quick.

It is no accident that most of the popular application programs are highly interactive. For example, when you delete a word or change the page width in a word processing program, you see the results immediately. Similarly, when you change a number or formula in a spreadsheet, you see the results recalculated right away. When you perform a search or sort in a database, you also see the results immediately. This immediate feedback is what makes such programs highly interactive and useful.

The simple frequency of user response is probably not a good measure of interactivity. Response rate does not reveal the complexity of interaction involved. For example, a data entry program that involves 20 standard entries in a 15 minute period would generally not be considered as interactive as a process control program that requires 20 parameter settings in the same time period. Different levels of response processing, user control, helps, and error handling are associated with these two types of interactive sequences.

The design time required for the different kinds of interactive sequences listed in Table 2-2 usually increases by orders of magnitude. This is because the number of alternatives to be taken into account and the amount of information needed increases geometrically as the interaction gets more complex. Thus, a context-sensitive help may take 10 times longer to create than a simple help and an intelligent tutor may take 100 times longer. Multiple choice and data entry programs normally take a fraction of the time required to create application, game or process control software. So the sophistication of the interaction has important design and development implications.

Branching

Interactivity is produced by some form of branching within a program. A branch instruction tells the computer to go to one part of the program if one response is given and another place if a different response is given. While it is not important that you know how to write a branch instruction, it is important that you understand how branching works. When you design a program, you must be able to specify the logic of the interactive sequence via a flowchart or some other representational scheme. The critical aspect of the logic that you want to describe is the branching structure.

In this section, a number of different examples of branching are described. The first example shown in Figure 2-3 illustrates a sign-on sequence requiring the user to type an id and password.

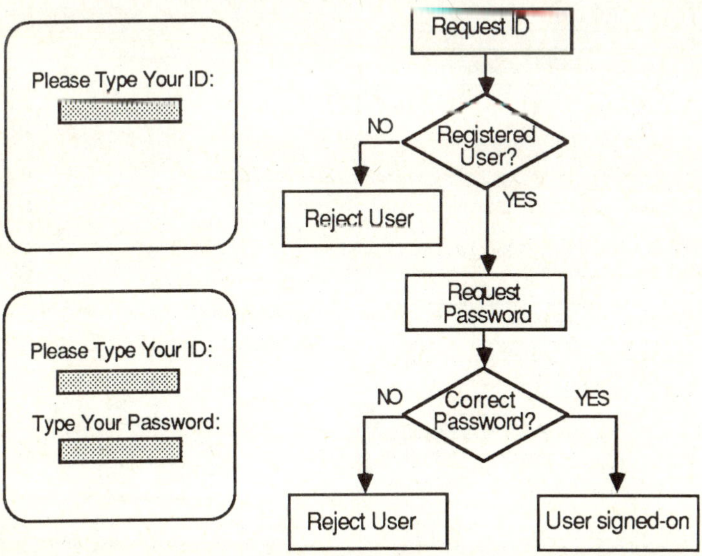

Figure 2-3

The display screens are shown on the left and the branching logic is on the right side. The diamond-shaped boxes indicate a branch and represent the response processing associated with user input. The program logic works as follows. If the user types in an invalid id, the system produces an "Invalid ID" message. If the ID is registered, the system asks for the password. If the password is correct, the user is signed on. If the password is incorrect, an "Invalid Password" message is displayed. This branching logic is typical of any data entry sequence. (This example is further discussed in Chapter 9.)

The second example is a multiple choice question with three response options (see Figure 2-4). The branching in this example involves the selection of one of the three possible feedback messages. This type of branching structure would be found in any question or menu sequence.

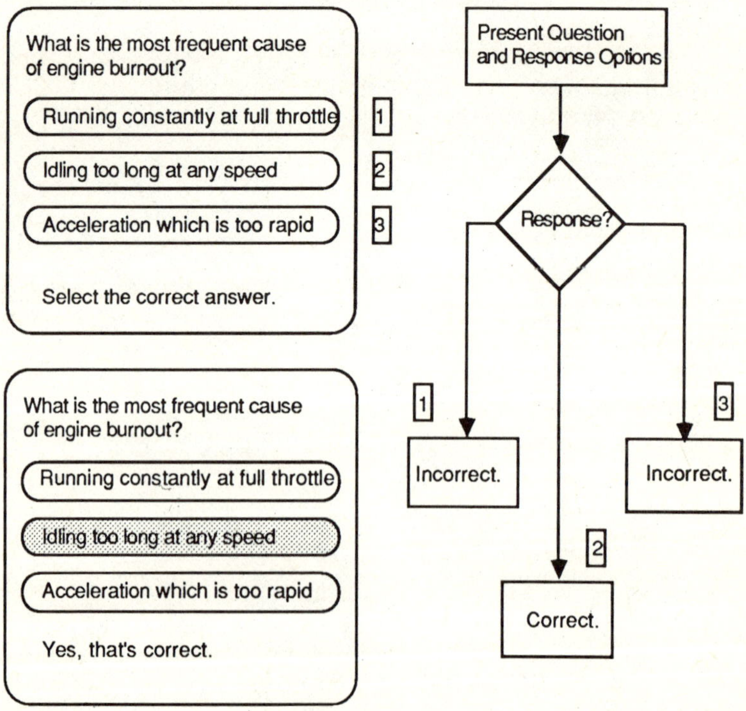

Figure 2-4

The third example illustrates the kind of branching that would be found in a game, simulation or process control program (see Figure 2-5). It involves a variable type of response. Imagine a stickshift that controls the speed of a motor. As the stickshift is moved from the KILL to the FULL throttle position and back via some form of pointing input, the speed of the motor increases or decreases. Speed is shown by the reading of the dial in revolutions per minute (rpm). The throttle and dial are shown on the left in the figure. The branching structure for this sequence is shown on the right.

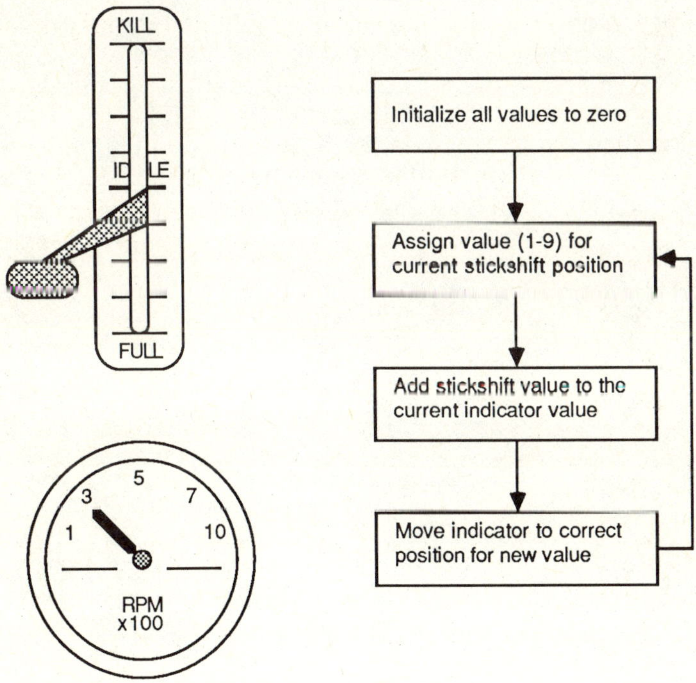

Figure 2-5

Here is how the branching logic works. The position (1-9) that the stickshift is moved to by the user is translated into a value between -4 to 4. The IDLE position corresponds to 0. Every second, the indicator on the dial is moved the number of notches given by the value (positive values are forward; negative values are backward). This is the loop shown between the last box and the second box in the flowchart. Since there are 4 notches for each 100 rpm (not shown on the dial), it would take 10 seconds to reach 1000 rpm if the throttle is put into FULL position. When the stickshift is put in the IDLE position, the value is 0 so the indicator stays at its current position on the dial. Note that in the beginning, the indicator will not start to move until the stickshift is past the idle position. Also note that any rpm value below 0 or above 10 will not move the indicator beyond the initial or final positions on the dial.

The fourth example of branching is an intelligent advisor or tutor for a program involving the throttle sequence in the preceding example and the diagnostic knowledge of the first example. The purpose of this segment is to detect a user who frequently idles and warn them that this may result in engine burnout. The logic for the program is shown in the flowchart on the right of Figure 2-6. The advice generated when the problem is detected is shown in the screen on the left of the figure.

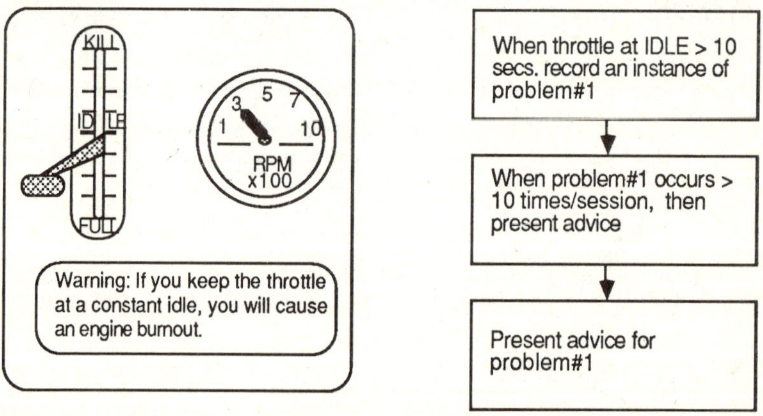

Figure 2-6

Note that the advice is only generated after the idling behavior is shown 10 times in a session. Thus, the advisor looks for patterns of behavior rather than single responses.

The last example illustrates multiple input processing. Figure 2-7 shows a typical spreadsheet. This spreadsheet has a menu bar at the top and function key prompts at the bottom of the screen. The user moves around the spreadsheet using arrow keys. Commands in the menu bar are also selected via the arrow keys.

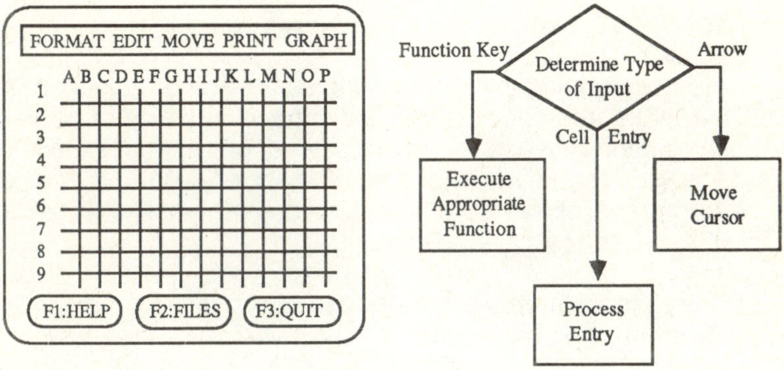

Figure 2-7

At any one time, the user could press a function key, an arrow key to move the cursor, or enter cell information such as data or a formula. Each one of these inputs leads to further processing. If a function key is pressed, the appropriate function will be executed. If the cursor is moved into the menu bar and followed by Enter, the appropriate command is executed. If a cell entry is made, this will be processed accordingly. There is a considerable amount of error handling associated with response processing for this type of program (see discussion in Chapter 9).

These five examples illustrate differences in branching structures for different response levels and interactive sequences. The first example shows branching based upon data (sign-on id and password) entered by the user. In the second example, the branching determines which feedback message is displayed and depends upon which answer is selected. In the third example, the branching determines the movement of a dial indicator and depends upon the position of the throttle stickshift.

In example four, the branching determines when (and if) certain advice is given and depends upon whether the stickshift is kept in an idle position frequently. In the spreadsheet example, the branching depends upon what kind of input is made. The branching logic in each successive example is more complex and results in a more sophisticated degree of interactivity.

Response Data

Interaction between people involves an exchange of information. We make inferences and draw conclusions on the basis of the information revealed. A well designed program does this too. In fact, the recording and use of response data is one of the characteristics of interactive software that distinguishes it from other types of programs.

Every time you make a response when using a computer, this response can be recorded. This includes menu selections, answers to questions and any sequence of key presses or pointing actions made. Time durations can also be measured. For example, the time taken to go through a unit can be recorded and used to estimate the difficulty in understanding the material presented. The time taken to provide an answer to a question (response latency) can also be measured and used to assess how well the person knows the answer.

The response data collected is used to make branching decisions as outlined in the previous section. There are basically four kinds of branching criteria: exact match, counters, vectors, and knowledge networks. A branch based upon an exact match requires that the user response be exactly the same as a pre-specified string, number or keypress. The sign-on example (Figure 2-3) and the spreadsheet example (Figure 2-7) illustrate this type of branching. With counters, a branching decision is made on the basis of the value of a single variable. For example, here is a set of branching rules based upon a counter ERRORS which keeps track of the total number of errors made in a unit:

If ERRORS $\leq$ 2 then go to unit 24
If ERRORS >2 and $\leq$ 4 then go to unit 21
If ERRORS > 4 then repeat this unit

With vectors, the branching decision is made on the basis of a pattern of responses. For example, suppose the user has just completed a financial planning analysis consisting of seven questions, each with three alternatives. The following set of rules might be used to determine what investment options the person should consider based upon their answers to the questions:

If answers = {a,c,b,a,a,a,c} then options 1,2,3,5,8,9
If answers = {a,c,a,c,b,b,a} then options 1,2,3,7,8,9,10
If answers = {b,c,a,a,a,c,a} then options 1,3,8,10

Clearly the use of vectors allows for many possible branching paths. In the example just described, there would be over 2000 possible alternatives (7 questions with 3 choices each). It is likely that only a small subset of these alternatives would be used.

With knowledge networks, branching decisions are made on the basis of matching concepts or diagnosing misconceptions. Normally, this will involve natural language understanding capability and the use of artificial intelligence programming techniques. For example, consider the following branching rules that might be found in an intelligent advisor program for a nuclear plant technician:

If answer = {warning switch 5 is on} then recommend procedure 4A
If answer = {don't know} then explain {gauge reading procedure}
If answer = {temperature is steady} then ask about {pressure}

In the first rule, if the answer contains the concept that a particular warning switch is on, then a specific procedure is recommended. However, if the technician does not know how to answer, then the advisor needs to explain how to read a gauge. If the answer indicates that temperature is steady, it is necessary to ask for a pressure reading. Note that natural language understanding capability will be needed to determine if the answers provided match the concepts referenced in the rules.

We have been discussing the use of response data for branching. Response data is also important in analyzing the effectiveness of a program and deciding what revisions are needed. This will be discussed at length in Chapter 10.

2/ Interactivity

Summary

There are a number of different ways of defining interactivity. Interactivity is a function of the levels of response involved in a program and the types of interactive sequences used. Different levels of response include single key presses, multiple choice selections, words or expressions, multiple responses, and natural language/speech input. Different types of interactive sequences include multiple choice options/questions, data entry, helps, applications programs, simulations/games, process control and intelligent tutors /advisors.

Interactivity is produced by means of branching. Five different examples of branching were examined in the chapter: a sign-on sequence, a multiple choice question, an indicator controlled by a stickshift, an intelligent advisor and a spreadsheet.

User responses are the basis for making branching decisions. Four types of decision criteria which can be used for branching are exact matches, counters, vectors, and knowledge networks.

3/ Development Process

Software development is a complex process consisting of a number of steps. This chapter discusses some of the major steps including requirements, specifications, prototypes, and pilot testing. Different approaches to development, the relationship between design and programming, and factors affecting development time/costs are also discussed.

Development Approaches

There are many different approaches to creating software. Let's compare two scenarios that represent different ends of the development spectrum: a college instructor versus a software production team.

The college instructor works as a lone artist, handcrafting the program and making all decisions on the basis of intuition and personal teaching experience. Most of the development is done in the evenings and on weekends; there is no development schedule or target completion date. An authoring system is used to produce completed lessons without any need for programming. The authoring system includes a graphics editor which allows the instructor to draw all graphics.

The production team belongs to a commercial software development company and must turn out good quality programs according to a specification, schedule and budget. Table 3-1 lists the team composition.

Table 3-1

Software Production Team
Software Engineer
System Analyst
Programmer
Graphics Designer
Editor
Project Manager
Evaluation Specialist

All of the team members work on a number of projects simultaneously. The role of the project manager is to coordinate the work of all the team members and keep the development on schedule and on budget. The team follows well defined procedures for each step of the development process.

A standard programming language is used by the programmer to code the program. Graphics are created by the graphics designer using a graphics editor which produces files to be integrated into the program by the programmer. The software undergoes extensive usability testing and revision.

Despite the major differences between these two development approaches, the resulting programs could be very good (or very bad). The critical factor is not the approach used, but the extent to which the design principles described in the next part of this book are followed. If the single author or the production team has extensive experience designing interactive software, this will determine the quality of the programs produced.

The two cases just described represent two extremes. Software can be developed by groups of any size and with various backgrounds. Most commercially available software is developed by members of a software engineering team. However, individuals often develop outstanding programs; many famous programs have been developed by one person working alone. To summarize, there is no right or wrong approach to software development.

Requirements

Any software development project begins with some form of requirements analysis. To design a good program it is absolutely essential to know what the user wants (and doesn't want). Requirements can be approached from a number of different perspectives: functional, technical, and marketing. Functional requirements specify what the program must do; technical requirements indicate how the program must work; and marketing requirements describe what is needed for the program to be purchased.

While it is conceivable that software designers or the design team may be able to define the requirements from their own experience and knowledge, it is normal to collect data to define requirements. There are many techniques used to do this. The most common methodology is *task analysis*. Task analysis involves studying what people do when they perform a task, the mistakes they make, and success/failure criteria. A very detailed representation of the task is constructed with particular attention to performance measures (e.g., completion times, frequency). From this information, it is possible to develop a good idea of what features are needed in a program to help the user carry out the task.

Another technique commonly used to define requirements is the use of *focus groups*. A focus group is a small group of people who are selected because they are typical of the expected users of a program. They are presented with various descriptions of the program (possibly including mocked up screens) and their reactions measured. Focus groups provide a good opportunity to explore various design alternatives with users very early in the development process.

One of the most important aspects of defining requirements is achieving a good understanding of the user. Knowing how the user is likely to react to different aspects of the program, helps you make good design decisions about screen displays, user control, response processing, error handling, and so on.

Defining user requirements is a major focus of human factors engineering. See the references to human factors research in Appendix B.

Specifications

Regardless of what kind of development approach is followed, one critical component of the development process is good documentation of the design, i.e., specifications. While it is possible to do all development directly at the terminal, this is very unlikely given the complexity of interactive software.

Furthermore, when working in any kind of team arrangement, or when approval or review of a design is needed, it is necessary to have the program documented in some fashion so that its design can be communicated. Two levels of specifications are needed: functional specifications and programming specifications.

Functional specifications describe the overall structure and operation of the program in terms of input, output, and processes. They also describe the assumptions made in the design of the program about the intended user, hardware and software capabilities, performance factors, etc. Functional specifications usually include diagrams showing the inter-relationship of all functions and data files.

Programming specifications are much more detailed and include descriptions of display formats, input/output sequences, data files, and all branching logic. Branching logic is often described in the form of flowcharts, decision tables, or data flow diagrams. Martin & McClure (1985) provide a good overview of the various techniques used to diagram program structure and logic.

Specifications represent the blueprints for a program. The functional specifications are used by software designers to describe how a program will work (independent of how it is implemented). They can be used by reviewers to approve or suggest changes to the program before it is actually written. Programming specifications are used by programmers to create the program.

> Transportability of programs across different systems is a major issue in the software domain. After spending a lot of time and money developing a program, it is desirable to have it run on as many different computers as possible. The problem is that a program developed for one machine is not likely to run on a different machine. One solution to this problem is to use programming or authoring languages which are available for a wide variety of machines. However, in many cases, it will be necessary to rewrite the program from the specifications using a different language or system. In such cases, specifications play an important role in transportability.

Prototypes

While specifications provide a detailed description of the program, they do not convey the interactive or dynamic aspects very well. It is very difficult to visualize exactly how a program will work from the specifications. For this reason, it is highly desirable to create prototypes as part of the design step.

A prototype is a working model or mock-up of the actual program. It is only a small part of the entire program and usually contains a few displays or sequences which are representative. While the prototype works, it may not work in the same way as the real program will. For example, a function which graphs data may display a stored graph instead of actually generating one from the input provided, animation may be represented by a few discrete screens instead of a full sequence, or only some of the feedback messages for a response are implemented. The challenge in building a prototype is to create enough of the program to illustrate how it will work, but do as little actual programming as possible.

In addition to the purpose of showing what a program will be like when it is completed, another function of a prototype is to assess how difficult it will be to program certain sequences. It is often difficult to estimate how long it will take to program something that has not been done before. Implementing these sequences in a prototype allows a more accurate estimate of how long the full design will take.

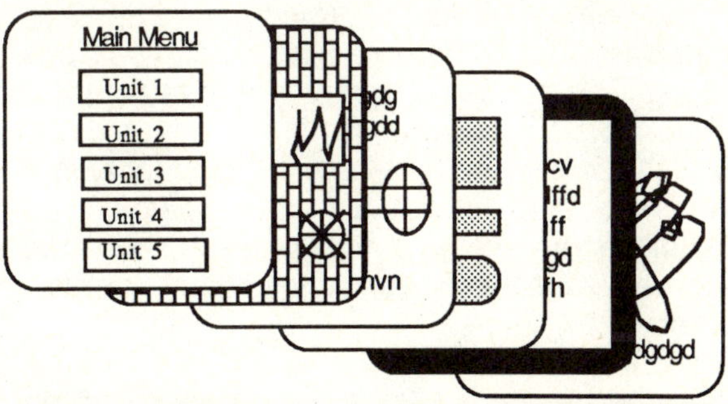

A prototype should contain a sample of everything in the program.

The best way to decide what should go into a prototype is to go through the completed specifications and select examples of sequences which are very common or very unusual. You may want to include a complete unit or segments from many units. At most, a prototype should contain no more than 10 percent of the entire program.

Pilot Testing

No matter how well a design was thought out and how carefully it was programmed, there will still be many things that have been overlooked. This includes unexpected responses, missing examples, ambiguous directions, explanations that are unclear, additional helps that are needed, and so on. All of these flaws will result in user problems with the program. The purpose of pilot testing is to discover these flaws.

There are lots of ways to do pilot tests. They can be done as one-on-one tryouts where the evaluator sits with the user and observes the problems that occur. The tryout may be video-taped for detailed analysis after the session. Alternatively, the program can be tested with a group of users who fill out questionnaires after they have completed the tryout. Questionnaires or the capability to make comments can be built into the tryout program so that users can provide feedback as they actually go through it.

While some of these methods provide more detailed or accurate data than others, any form of pilot testing will produce useful information. The more pilot testing you can do, the better. Each new person who tries out the program may reveal a problem or weakness that everyone else had missed. Because the only way to get programs bug-free is trial and error, you need lots of trials to find all the errors. Generally, pilot testing should be continued until you have met the performance requirements specified for the program.

One of the problems in pilot testing is deciding when to make changes that deal with preferences rather than errors. A simple rule of thumb is as follows: make changes suggested by only one person when they seem like major improvements, give serious consideration to any changes suggested by two different individuals, and always makes changes suggested by three or more people (no matter what you think!). By using objective performance data such as response time or errors, you can reduce the need to rely on preference data. In Chapter 10, we will discuss more formal methods of analyzing response data which can also be used in pilot testing.

Development Time

One of the most asked questions about the development of interactive software is "How long does it take to develop a program?" This question is analogous to the question "How long does it take to build a house?" Both questions have the same answer: "It depends."

It depends on how fancy you want your program to be, how big, and how fast you want it built. It also depends upon the experience of the designer (or development team), the extent to which the functions already exist in some form, and the programming tools used. These factors can account for an order of magnitude difference in development time.

Experienced designers may be able to develop a program in half the time required by inexperienced designers (since they are familiar with the principles outlined in this book). Some programming systems can reduce the development time by as much as 40 percent relative to the use of a programming language. If the content already exists in online or offline form, up to 50 percent of the development time may be saved compared to creating the program for something totally new. If we combine these three time savings, we could theoretically reduce the development time for a program by 90 percent! In practice, some aspects of design (such as quality review and revision) tend to be a constant for a program of a given type and size.

Another factor to keep in mind is that each additional display or presentation feature you use (e.g., windowing, color, graphics, sound, speech, video), will increase the development time (see Figure 3-2). Each feature has to be thought about, programmed, debugged, and tested. The design dilemma is that you can create a simple program quickly or take a lot longer for a fancy one.

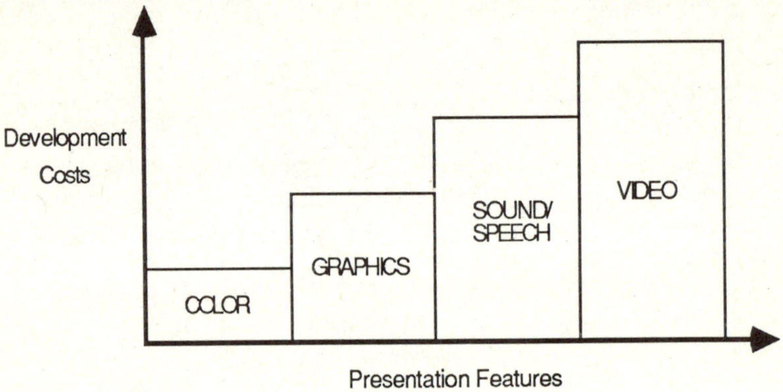

Figure 3-2

The development time also depends upon the level of quality desired. If all of the elements of quality mentioned in Chapter 1 are to be included in a program, this will require a lot more development time than if only a few are taken into account. An explicit decision about the level of quality desired for a program is made by specifying what elements will/will not be included.

There are some important practical rules that you can derive from the preceding discussion. The development time (and costs) of software will be minimized if:

1) the program is based upon something that already exists
2) the designers have experience creating interactive software
3) powerful programming tools are used
4) simple presentation strategies are used
5) the level of quality desired is moderate

In most situations, you will not have control over all of these factors. However, you are likely to have control over some of them and this gives you an opportunity to reduce development time and costs.

Relationship Between Design and Programming

A perennial issue in software development is the relationship between design and programming. Even though design and programming activities are separate aspects of developing software, they are closely intertwined. For example, programming specifications are derived from the functional specifications but programming considerations often result in changes to the design.

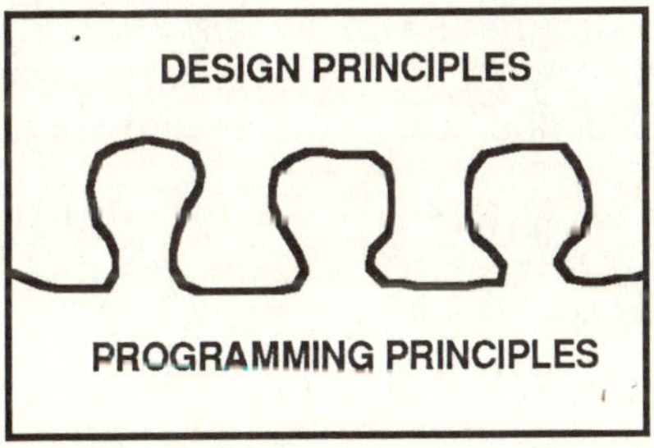

Design and programming principles are closely interrelated.

There are programming principles that should be applied to the implementation of a program to achieve satisfactory performance, reliability, and maintainability. Examples include:

- Use subroutines whenever possible
- Pass arguments between subroutines instead of using global variables
- Use case constructs (IF-THEN-ELSE)
- Keep data distinct from logic
- Use variables rather than constants
- Locate all data and variable definitions in one place
- Regenerate rather than store

Such programming principles are complementary to the design guidelines outlined in this book. In some areas, there is considerable overlap between design guidelines and programming principles (e.g., error handling, documentation). In other areas, there is relatively little overlap (such as screen design and response processing).

Summary

Development approaches can range from a single individual doing all aspects of design and development to a team consisting of many members. The experience of the designer(s) creating interactive software is the most important factor determining the success of the development approach.

Two levels of specifications are needed to properly document the design of a program. Functional specifications describe the structure and operation of the program. Programming specifications describe how to implement the program.

Prototypes are important in the design process because they provide a concrete example of what the program will look like and how it will work. A prototype should consist of a sample of critical elements of the program.

Pilot testing is critical to finding flaws in programs. Pilot tests can be conducted one-on-one or in groups. Data can be collected by observation or by having participants complete online or offline questionnaires. The more pilot testing conducted, the better.

The amount of time required to develop a program depends upon a number of factors, including i) the experience of the designer(s), ii) the extent to which the content already exists, iii) the programming tools used, iv) the presentation features involved and v) the quality desired.

Design guidelines and programming principles are complementary. Both should be followed to produce good quality software.

4/ Software Support

Some form of user support will be needed for almost all software. This support typically takes the form of reference tools, training tools, job aids, and telephone hotlines. Together, these support materials are an important aspect of a software product's success. Even a well designed program may fail if it is poorly supported. This chapter discusses the various forms of user support that can be provided.

Reference Tools

Reference tools are consulted by users to find answers to a specific problem or review something they have previously learned. Although many users use reference materials as learning materials, this is not their main purpose.

Some common reference tools are *Reference Manuals, User Guides,* and *Quick Reference Cards.* Quick reference cards fall into middle ground between reference tools and job aids, and they will be discussed as job aids. Reference information can also be provided as online files.

Reference Manuals

The primary reference document for a software product is the reference manual. This text provides "everything you always wanted to know " about a program, usually divided by subtopics such as "Search Commands" or "Printer Configurations". The purpose of the reference manual is to provide a source for the user to solve a particular problem or learn more about a specific capability of the program.

The primary design consideration with a reference manual is easy accessibility of information. This means that it should be clearly organized. Typically, reference manuals are organized alphabetically by program functions. In a command-based program, for example, the manual would be organized around the command names (e.g., SEARCH, SORT, MERGE, CALCULATE).

In a reference manual, the table of contents and index must provide detailed cross references. The index, especially, should list topics as many different ways as the user might search for the topic. Some suggestions are: (1) by name (e.g., CREATE), (2) by alias (e.g., "New File"), and (3) by function (e.g., "document files, creating them").

Reference manuals should provide detailed information on the steps in each procedure and the available options for each function in a program. The step-by-step instructions should be augmented with illustrations and examples as much as possible. Special attention should be paid to likely problems and their solutions. Reference manuals can further assist the novice user by ensuring that important terms are defined as they are used and by providing a glossary.

User Guides

User guides are documents which cover special aspects of system use. These guides are especially useful for procedures which are not repeated often enough to warrant the user learning the procedures. An installation guide, for example, presents step-by-step procedures showing users how to set up their system. The steps cover every action required by the user to get their system running. This often includes configuration instructions for different peripherals and instructions on how to prepare back-up copies of diskettes.

Other common types of user guides are troubleshooting guides (i.e., procedures to follow to diagnose and correct problems), application guides (specific instructions that explain how to use a program for a particular application), coordinator guides (steps to follow to coordinate or supervise the use of software by a number of people), and sales guides (techniques to be used to sell a particular software product).

User guides should present an easily followed sequence of steps, illustrated by photographs or examples of user input and system output. The steps are often numbered to make them easier to follow.

Online Reference Files

It is becoming common practice to provide reference documents as text files on the same disk as the program. This ensures that the documentation is always distributed at the same time as the program and (hopefully) that it is current. The user can print out the documentation as it is needed or just read it on the screen. Furthermore, users can use the search capability of any word processor to find specific terms. They can also create their own reference document by copying the text to a new file and reorganizing it to suit their needs.

Training Tools

Training tools take the form of tutorials, training packages, or seminars/workshops. Ironically, print is the most common format for teaching people how to use software. Print is relatively inexpensive to produce, takes minimum development time, and can be highly flexible. Furthermore, it is a medium that most users are very comfortable with. It is much easier to find writers and printing companies than it is to find programmers and software development firms. However, the development of programming systems that require minimal computer background is making the development of computer-based learning materials much more feasible.

Users handle training materials differently depending on their experience and need. The novice user might proceed through a tutorial linearly, doing the sections in order and learning the system in detail. The very experienced user may want to use tutorial materials solely as a reference tool, looking up only those aspects of the system use they can't remember or about which they aren't clear. The intermediate user tends to use training materials both ways, as reference tool for skills they need to review and as a tutorial for new features they are mastering.

You can use color, boxes, emphasis, and other formatting techniques to help differentiate explanatory information from core materials. This will allow more experienced users to go through the training materials at a more rapid pace and will still provide the explanations and examples required by the beginning user.

Tutorials

Tutorials are designed to teach the user how to use the software by means of detailed explanations, examples, illustrations and practice exercises. This contrasts with reference manuals which are intended for review and consultation, or user guides which describe a specific procedure.

Tutorials are generally conversational in tone and provide specific feedback for each activity or exercise so a user can determine if they are learning correctly. When the user is asked to do something there should be a description of all the likely error conditions as well as the expected result. For example:

> **Select the F1 function key to see the updated amount.**
> If you accidently press a different key, press F1 again.
> If pressing F1 doesn't work, press the ESC key and select the RESUME option, then press F1.

Clearly, the extent to which you can suggest proper recovery procedures depends upon how the software is designed. Some software makes recovery difficult because it does not handle errors well (see Chapter 9).

Tutorial lessons should be short to minimize the amount to be learned at any one time. Also, the lessons should be as independent as possible since you can't assume that the user will necessarily take the lessons in the order presented or suggested. Tutorials should make use of realistic examples. If the users can easily see how mastering a skill will help them solve a real problem, it will help motivate them to continue to learn.

The two most typical problems that users have with training materials are (1) knowing when to actually do something and (2) getting lost after doing something on the system. When people are learning to use a computer, they generally have an action orientation. This means that they want to try something as soon as they read about it. In addition, many manuals do not clearly distinguish between describing something and having the user try it. This frequently causes a problem because the user will try something before it has been properly explained, or they will fail to do something when they are expected to do so.

To avoid this problem, it is critical to have a way to distinguish explanations from instructions to do something. This can be achieved by always stating actions as imperatives (e.g., Type the following...) and using color, highlighting, italics or some other cueing technique to signify when an action is required.

People often get lost after a hands-on activity because they forget where they left off in the training materials. To avoid this problem, it is desirable to place hands-on activities at the end of a lesson. After completing the activity, users begin a new section rather than having to try and find their place in the middle of a lesson. It is also desirable to put some sort of identifier on the screen (e.g., Exercise 4) to remind people where they are. The best aid is a prompt message on the system that tells the user to go back to the documentation and continue reading at a certain page or section. This is an example of how printed documentation and the system need to be designed together in order to work well.

Illustrations of screen displays help users locate themselves and provide confidence that they are on the right track. Good software tutorials make extensive use of screen illustrations. Of course, not every screen can be shown. The most frequently used displays and menu screens should be selected.

A slight problem with using screen displays is that they tend to change with each different version of the program. Small discrepancies do not seem to bother users significantly. On the other hand, this could be a major source of confusion to users.

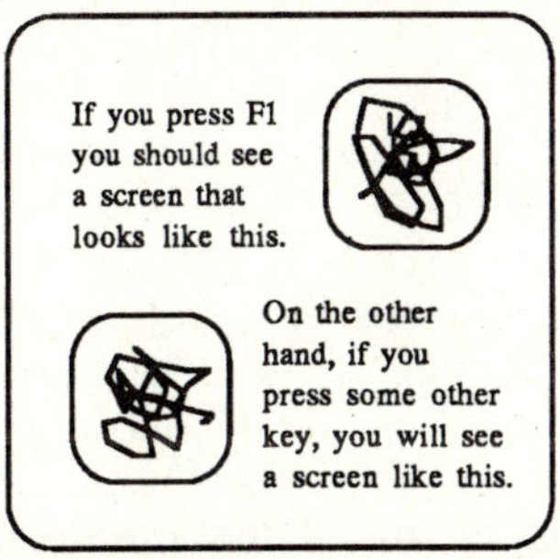

Illustrate documentation with screen displays.

Traditionally, tutorials have been developed to teach all the features and capabilities of a program. However, most users only use the tutorials while they are becoming acquainted with the program. After they have mastered the basic skills needed to operate the program, they tend to rely on the reference materials (or trial and error) to obtain further information. This suggests that tutorials are best used for teaching the basics of a program rather than the advanced features.

At the very least, the basic and advanced features can be put in separate tutorials for use at different times or with different levels of users. This will allow you to design each document to more specifically reflect the anticipated experience level of the users.

Many software vendors now provide an introductory tutorial to teach the minimum set of skills needed to use the program. These tutorials have names such as QuickStart™ (Visicorp) or Fast Track™ (DayFlo). They are designed to get a new user, especially novice computer users, successfully using the product within an hour or less. For example, an introductory tutorial for a word processing program might cover how to create a new document, print it, and save it. The user should be able to learn to do this in 20 to 30 minutes.

A basic skills tutorial for a product provides instruction on the routine functions that most people will use. It does not go into every nuance of each function, but teaches only the essential features or capabilities of the program. It's comparable to giving someone a conversational grasp of a foreign language via a phrase book instead of teaching them the full structure of the language.

A third form of tutorial is an applications tutorial that teaches how to use a product for a specific work application. An application tutorial is similar to an application guide, except that the tutorial is intended to teach whereas the guide is not. An applications tutorial will teach advanced features or particular combinations of features needed for a given application. For example, a word processing program might have applications tutorials for producing legal forms, technical documents, or repetitive letters.

These different types of tutorials match differences in user backgrounds, work requirements and learning styles. They also make it easier to revise and update the product documentation. As new features are added to the product, or new applications are developed, they can be added as supplemental materials that build on the existing tutorials.

Until recently, tutorials were always provided in printed form. Now, many tutorials are provided in online form as computer-based instruction. This approach is currently more expensive to develop than print but it allows the tutorial to be uniquely tailored to the needs of each user (i.e., individualized instruction). Some people feel the instructional advantages outweigh the additional development cost. Appendix B provides references to the design of computer-based instruction.

Multimedia Packages

Some vendors develop multimedia training packages for their products. These can take the form of audio or video cassettes (also videodisc). Multimedia training packages provide audio or visual cues to help users learn how to use the software. This additional source of information may make the learning more effective and more interesting.

Pacing, interaction, and indexing are potential problem areas with multimedia materials. In self-teaching situations, the learner must have control of the pace. Audio or video materials that move too quickly or too slowly lose instructional effectiveness. Even though learners can theoretically stop and review materials as often as they wish, in practice this tends to be too cumbersome with most audio and video equipment. Print materials allow the user to pace themselves easily and repeat each portion of the instruction as often as they wish. This is also a capability of well designed online instruction.

Another potential problem with audio or video materials is keeping the user synchronized between what they are doing on the computer and what they are doing with the training materials. It is common for learners to "get lost" going back and forth between computer activites and the audio/video materials. For this reason, special care must be taken to direct the user to the appropriate materials at any point in the tutorial.

When a user wants specific information in a text, they can go to the index. With audiovisual media, this presents a problem since there is nothing equivalent to an index. Specific tape locations can be provided but this requires that the tape counter is accurately set to locate sequences properly. Videodisc materials can be indexed like a text, although these indices are not always as easy to use as a book index.

In choosing to use multimedia materials, the instructional advantages must be weighed against the potential disadvantages described. With good design, these disadvantages can be minimized, resulting in very effective training materials.

Workshops/Seminars

Workshops or seminars are a common way to provide software training, especially for more complex programs. These courses provide experts to train users in small groups, usually with "live" demonstrations and hands-on practice.

Workshops have a number of advantages and disadvantages. They provide an opportunity for users to receive one-on-one help from an expert and interact with other users. The demonstrations and hands-on practice are usually considered very effective ways to learn.

On the other hand, the quality of workshops varies with the quality of the instructor (not all experts are good teachers!). The biggest disadvantage of workshops is that they are usually expensive and require time away from the job. This is the main reason why most software training is provided in print form rather than via workshops.

Job Aids

A job aid is a concise summary of the functions or procedures associated with a software product. Job aids can be presented in offline or online formats. Offline job aids take the form of quick reference cards or keyboard templates. Online job aids usually take the form of help screens. An expert system can provide a sophisticated online help capability.

Quick reference cards

Quick reference cards are usually pocket-sized sheets of cardboard that list all the commands or functions of the program. They serve as a memory aid to remind the user what the correct format of the commands or key presses are. They provide no explanations.

Keyboard templates

Keyboard templates can take two forms. One form is really just a quick reference card that fits over or on the keyboard. The other kind of template is key specific. It identifies the functions associated with each key. For example, a function key template could fit over the function keys and identify the operation(s) associated with each function key.

> Actually, job aids can come in a lot of interesting forms. For example, TechNovelty Inc. of Dublin, Ohio markets an MS-DOS Coffee Mug. The mug has the full set of MS DOS commands written on it. As long as you have your coffee mug handy, you can check the correct name or fomat of a DOS command.

Online Helps

The most common form of online helps are sets of screens that contain explanations of specific functions. The help may be called up by use of a designated function key, by typing a help command, or by choosing a help option from a menu. Online helps may provide static information which is independent of what the user is doing, or they may be context-sensitive and provide different information depending upon where and how they are invoked. Different levels of helps may be provided that provide successively more detailed information.

Chapter 8 discusses the design of online helps further.

Expert Systems

An expert system is a program that uses expert judgements to provide advice for specific situations. Expert systems are a relatively new development in software based upon artificial intelligence research.

An expert system could provide a very sophisticated form of online help since it is based upon considerable knowledge of an application or program. For example, an expert system could be developed for an applications software program and would be able to give the user advice on how to use the program for what they want to accomplish.

At the current time, expert systems are very expensive to develop and would only make sense as job aids for large and complex software systems. However, in the future, it is likely that expert systems will become much less expensive to develop due to the availability of powerful programming environments. Appendix B provides references to the design of expert systems and the use of Artificial Intelligence techniques.

Telephone Hotlines

The last form of software support to be considered is the use of telephone hotlines that help users with problems or answer questions about programs. Hotlines are staffed by technical experts who are very familiar with the software and have experience helping users with problems.

Hotlines are a relatively easy way to provide high quality user support. However, it is often difficult to find people who are sufficiently knowledgeable about a program and who have the necessary skills and patience to help users via phone. From a user's perspective, it is usually important that the assistance be immediate since they are often unable to continue their work until their problem is resolved. For this reason, hotlines where immediate help is not available are not well accepted.

Hotlines are highly valuable to software developers since they provide a rich database of information about problems with the software and how people try to use the program (successfully and unsuccessfully). This information can be the basis for revisions and future enhancements.

Summary

The design of the support materials for a software program is as important as the design of the program itself. This includes reference tools, training tools, job aids, and hotlines. Without proper support, the user may not be able to use the software effectively. As the users become more familiar with the software, the way they use the software support materials changes. It is important to design support materials with the different levels of user experience in mind.

Reference tools take the form of reference manuals, user guides, online files, or quick reference cards. The most important characteristic of reference documents is that they be well organized so that information can be found easily by the user. Table 4-1 summarizes important features of documentation design discussed in this chapter.

Table 4-1

Document Design Considerations
Readability
Good Indexing
Logical Organization
Explanation of terms
Step-by-Step Instructions
Use of Illustrations
Use of Examples
Completeness
Consistency
Currentness

Training tools can be offline or online tutorials, multimedia materials, or workshops. Print materials tend to provide the least expensive and most flexible form of training, although online tutorials, multimedia packages and workshops all have certain advantages.

Job aids provide concise summaries of program functions. Offline job aids include quick reference cards and keyboard templates. Online job aids take the form of help displays. Expert systems can also provide a sophisticated form of job aids.

Telephone hotlines can provide specific help for user problems and questions. To be most efffective, hotlines must provide immediate assistance to users.

PART II:

GUIDELINES

5/ Displays

Display design is one of the most evident aspects of creating interactive software. Even though there are lots of other components to software, display screens are what people see and are often the primary factor used to judge the quality of programs. For this reason, a lot of attention should be given to the design of displays in a program.

Relative to the design of the printed page, the design of screens is much more complex. Actually, the design of printed pages is pretty complex but it is usually done by specialists (i.e., graphic designers and typographers). The author of a book does not usually have anything to do with the layout of pages or printing. It is normal, however, for authors of software to do the design of their own screens. In many cases, it would be better left in the hands of a professional screen designer.

It may help to begin our discussion of screen design by comparing it to the design of printed pages. Some of the major differences are as follows:

- Unlike blank space on a printed page, blank space on a screen doesn't cost anything. Only information (i.e., text graphics) is stored.

- The screen is a dynamic display medium. Text can appear anyplace at any time.

- There are capabilities such as blinking, highlighting, and sound effects, which can be used as attentional devices.

- You can control the rate at which information is displayed on the screen.

- The resolution of screen displays is usually inferior to print.

- Screen displays can usually be modified much faster than print.

The guidelines in this and subsequent chapters address these differences. This chapter specifically examines the most important aspects of screen design.

Types of Screens

Screens differ in terms of purpose. Some different types of screens are:

Data Entry - Intended to let people enter data into some form of database (e.g., reservation system). Usually consist of a series of fields on the screen.

Inquiry - Intended to let people retrieve information from a database (e.g., order status system).

Control - Allows users to monitor and operate equipment (e.g., refinery control panel).

Informational - Presents information requested by user (e.g., videotex system).

Calculation - Allows users to make numerical calculations (e.g., accounting program).

Editor - Allows users to create and modify information (e.g., word processing program).

Menu - Allows a user to select options in a program (e.g., function key menu).

Question/Answer - Allows you to answer questions (e.g., online survey).

Some screens involve combinations of these different types. For example, an informational screen may be combined with a calculation or question/answer screen in a tutorial program. Many customer inquiry systems combine data entry and inquiry on the same screens. In addition, the use of windows (discussed later in this chapter) allows different types of screens to be super-imposed on the same display.

It is important to understand that each type of screen serves a different purpose and therefore has slightly different design considerations. For example, the most important characteristic of a data entry screen is that it allows fast and errorless entry of data. The location and order of the data entry fields on the screen is paramount. On the other hand, with an editor screen, flexibility of data entry may be much more important than speed and correctness. Color and graphics may not be especially important in calculation or menu screens but critical in a control or informational screen.

It is beyond the scope of this book to describe the design considerations for each type of screen display. The general guidelines provided in this chapter will result in more effective displays for almost any type of program. Other sources of information should be consulted for application specific guidelines. Artwick (1985) describes principles of designing graphics displays. Galitz (1985) will be especially helpful if your primary interest is designing data entry screens. Heines (1984) discusses screen design for computer based instruction.

Crowded Screens

Since it does not cost anything to have blank space on a screen, there is no reason to crowd a lot of information into a single screen. Well designed screens present one major idea or transaction per screen. Too much information on the screen at the same time produces "information overload" for the user and increases the likelihood of errors.

As a general rule, put no more that 12-16 lines of text and 1 graphic per screen. Break text up into short paragraphs of 3 or 4 sentences each with a double space between them. If you use windows as recommended below, you should have no problem with crowded or cluttered screens.

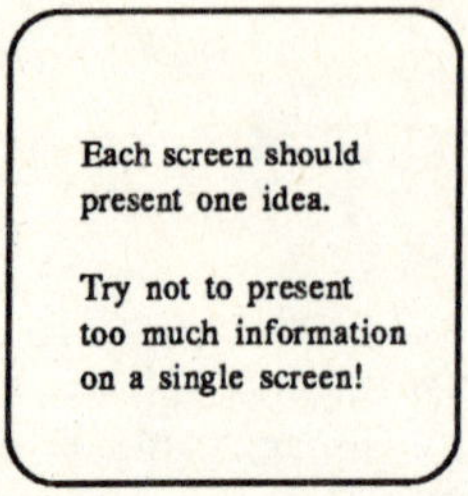

This...

...Not this.

An exception to these guidelines about limiting the amount of information on the screen are complex control displays or displays used for simulations or games. Another exception are data entry screens that have multiple fields to be filled in. In these cases, a lot of information may be packed on the screen. This is appropriate because all of the information on the screen needs to be kept together.

One important technique for minimizing screen clutter is to avoid displaying information until it is needed. Fields or control options that are not immediately needed are not displayed until later in the program. Pull-down windows (see below) are especially helpful in this respect.

Scrolling and Overlays

Since information can appear any place on the screen at any time, you have to make deliberate decisions about when to create a new screen and where to locate information. Unless you specifically create separate pages, information will continue to scroll from the bottom of the screen to the top. While scrolling may seem like a good idea, it quickly becomes very frustrating to the user. People tend to lose information as it rolls off the screen. It also becomes difficult for users to locate themselves in the program. For these reasons, always divide your program into separate pages. You may want to use use scrolling inside windows. In this case, provide a way for the user to scroll up and down (or left-right).

A second aspect of being able to display anything anywhere is the phenomenon of overlays. You have the capability to erase some portion of the screen and display something new on top of the old display, leaving everything else the same. The problem with overlays is that people often do not notice the new information that has been added. It is better to either create a new screen or use a window to introduce the new information. Overlays often save development time since they allow you reuse previous displays but possibly at the expense of user understanding.

Attentional Devices

Blinking (flashing), reverse video, highlighting (i.e., bold), and sound effects are devices which can be used to draw attention to something important on the screen. However, the value of these devices wears off quickly if they are overused and they become annoying to the user. As a general rule, use these devices sparingly and only use one of these devices per screen.

A special caution is associated with the use of sound. When you use sound effects, be aware that they may be disturbing to others in the vicinity of the terminal (unless headphones are used). For this reason, it is highly recommended that you provide an "off" option at the beginning of a program if you are using sound effects or speech output extensively. Of course, you will have to provide redundant cues that take the place of the turned off sound or speech.

Color

Color is another feature that can be used to capture attention. Historically, color has not been an important consideration in most software design applications because color displays were expensive and hence not very common. Some exceptions are video games, instructional software, and certain medical applications. However, the cost of color display hardware is dropping significantly and an increasing number of programs now use color displays. This includes business graphics, CAD/CAM, process control, and data entry programs.

Some general considerations for the use of color are as follows:

- Use color combinations that will always be discriminable (e.g., red & cyan, blue & yellow) and avoid using combinations such as blue & black or yellow & white.

- Code color redundantly with another cue such as size, patterns, labels.

- Outline images in a neutral border (e.g., black, grey, white) to facilitate edge discrimination.

- Use saturated colors to give the impression of size, weight or depth. Do not use saturated blue and red together unless depth is intended.

- Avoid using saturated blue for small images.

- Use certain color conventions such as red for emergency or yellow for caution. If colors are used for non-standard meanings, provide a legend.

- When using color for coding, do not use too many (i.e., more than about 5).

The appropriate use of color is application specific. Some different types of applications are:

Text: Color can be used to highlight misspellings or text to be cut/copied. It could also be used to indicate contributions by different authors or portions of text intended for different readers.

Functions: Color can be used to signify different functions. For example, in a windowing environment, each task or application program could use different color borders or backgrounds to help the user discriminate tasks/applications. Color could also be used in menus or data entry screens for the same purpose.

Charts/Graphs: Color can be used to help the user distinquish different variables or factors. Normally, less than 8 colors are needed.

Modeling: Color can be used to produce the illusion of depth. If realism is important, a large palatte of colors may be needed. Control of saturation levels and grey scale may be required.

Monitoring: Color is primarily used to attract attention. Examples include process control, medical systems, aircraft tracking, nuclear power plants, radar. Well chosen color combinations can be critical to human performance in life support situations.

Some practical considerations in using color are:

Hardware differences: Different monitors and interfaces will produce different colors. If the system configuration is not standardized and components can differ, the effects of careful color design will vary across different configurations (e.g., low versus high resolution monitors).

Monitor Adjustment: If the monitor is adjustable, individuals may adjust hue and intensity to suit their own preferences. This may reduce or destroy the intended effects of color.

Variations Across Output Devices: Printers/plotters produce colors that appear different than seen on the screen.

For further discussion of color in displays, see Smith (1987).

Windows

Because information is presented dynamically on a screen, it is important to help users organize it as much as possible. The best way to do this is to create windows (sometimes called viewports) for menus, questions, response or feedback areas, main concepts, examples, helps, etc. This makes it easier and faster for people to understand what they are reading/seeing.

A number of different kinds of windows are possible. The simplest type are fixed in location on the screen. On some machines (e.g., the Apple Macintosh™), windows can overlap

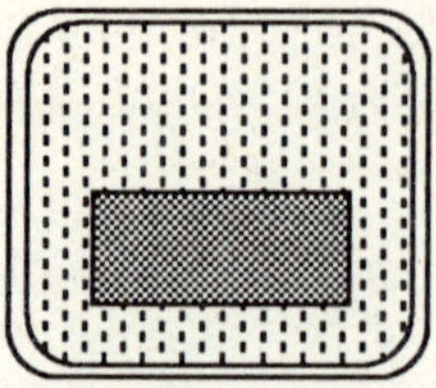

A fixed location or pop-up window

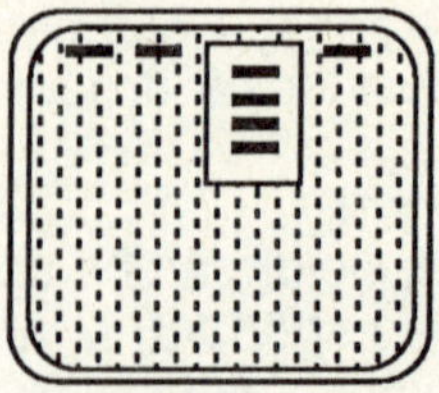

Pull-down window from a menu bar

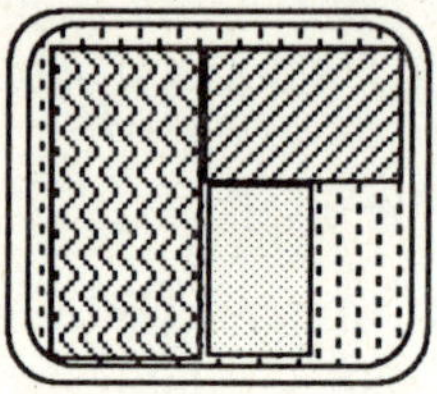

Tiled windows

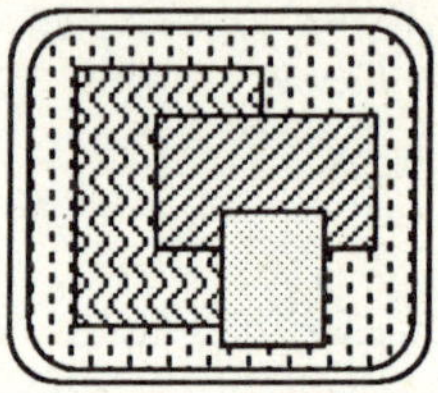

Overlapping windows

and be repositioned/resized by the user. In this case, the designer only has to worry about the default size and location of the window. On other machines, windows do not overlap but fit into the space available on the screen when activated (this is called *tiling*). In this case, the operating system determines the location and size of windows (however, the user can resize them).

Windows can be especially useful for menus or explanation (i.e., directions, helps). Pull down menus allow options to be hidden until the user selects a keyword from a menu bar. Similarly, pop-up windows (also called dialog boxes) provide prompts or options relevant to the current activity.

It is important to be consistent in the location and function of windows throughout a program. Do not present a question or directions in one part of a screen and then use the same location on a successive screen for a response or feedback area. While variety in screen design is important, create the variety within functions.

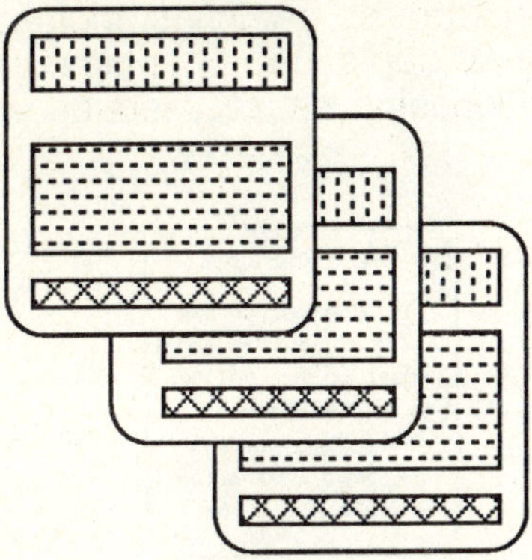

This...

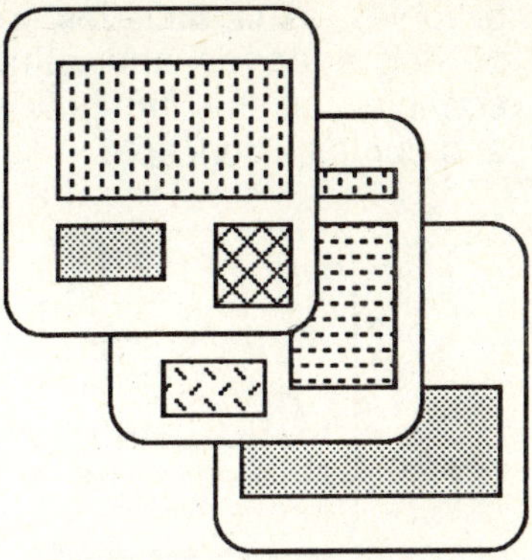

...Not This.

Different Type Sizes/Styles

Different sizes of type and different type styles (fonts) should be used for headings, labels, examples, questions, or any text that you want to stand out. This draws the attention of the user and makes the display more visually interesting. Examine any well designed book to see how different combinations of type sizes and styles can improve the readability of a document.

Of course, it is possible to overdo this. On systems where a wide selection of type styles and sizes are available, be careful not to use too many combinations on any particular screen. As a general rule, there should be a maximum of four different type styles/sizes per display. It is also important to be consistent in the use of type styles and sizes, i.e., all major headings should be the same style and size, etc.

Graphics

Illustrations usually convey ideas much faster and are more easily remembered than words. For these reasons, graphics should be used as much as possible. Even subject matter which is inherently alphanumeric (such as accounting, foreign languages, law) can be presented more effectively using graphics. This includes figures, diagrams, sketches, digitized photographs or any other visual depiction. Graphics are especially useful for showing relationships, causes, sequences, and complex concepts.

This...

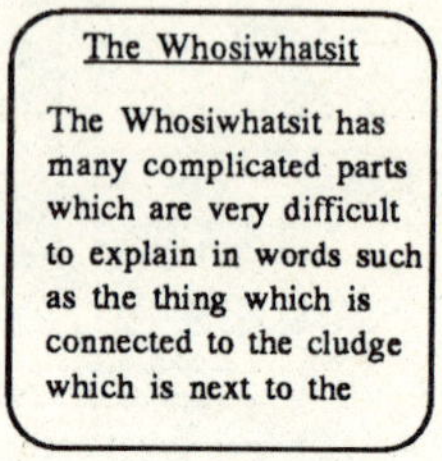

...Not This.

Note that graphics are not always self explanatory. Use labels or captions to explain a graphic. When using icons, you will probably need to provide an explanation of what each icon means. Also note that a high degree of realism or detail in graphics is usually not necessary or even desirable. In most cases, a line drawing is more effective than a full sketch or photograph.

One aspect of graphics use which is open for debate is the extent to which graphics should only be used when needed or for decorative purposes. Some people argue that graphics should only be used when they serve some real explanatory value. Others feel that graphics should be used to add aesthetic appeal to screen displays. This is not an idle argument since the creation of graphics take considerable time and skill. Each designer has to make their own decision about this point.

> The type of graphics possible will depend upon the display capabilities of the computer. The two major types of graphic displays are character and bit-mapped. With character displays you create your graphics in terms of individual characters which represent pieces of lines, curves, or symbols. With bit-mapped displays, you can address every point (called pixels) on the screen. Needless to say, you can draw much more detailed graphics with bit-mapped displays.

Animation represents a special graphics capability of computers (also possible with film/video). Animation involves moving objects or characters on the screen. It should be used to convey sequence or cause and effect. It can also be used simply as an attentional device.

Titles and Headings

One of the commonly reported problems with software is that users "get lost" and lose track of where they are (or were) in the program. This is because there are no inherent physical clues about location in a program (such as looking at how many pages are left in a book or the tape counter on a videocasette player). To overcome this problem, it is necessary to put titles or headings on screens so that users can easily identify their location. It may be sufficient to show the section or unit, or it may be desirable to number every screen, e.g.,

~~~~~~~~~~~~~~~~~ INTRODUCTION ~~~~~~~~~~~~~~~~ 5 / 16

Screen numbering works best with programs that are page oriented (i.e. not scrolling) However, headings can be used with any type of program.

A more sophisticated way of helping the user locate themselves is to provide some type of "map" or flowchart that shows them where they are in the program. This map should denote what parts of the program have been completed in the current session and which parts have not.

Display Resolution

A major factor which determines the degree of detail possible in a screen is the display resolution, i.e., how many individual points (pixels) on the screen can be addressed by the computer. The resolution of the display will determine how distinct text and graphics appear. It will also determine the range of type styles and size possible.

Ordinary television sets have relatively poor resolution (about
~~~~~~~~~~~~~~~~~

240 x 360 addressable points) whereas most computer monitors have higher resolution (about 600 x 400 addressable points). For comparison, a printed page has approximately 2000 x 2000 addressable points. The exact display resolution possible will depend upon the specific monitor and graphics display interface used.

As a designer, your challenge is to produce the most functional and attractive screens possible given the degree of display resolution available. If you follow the design guidelines outlined in this chapter, you will be able to develop effective screens regardless of the characteristics of the computer or monitor used.

Summary

Here are the points made in this chapter about display design:

- Do not crowd screens.
- Avoid the use of scrolling and overlays.
- Use attentional devices sparingly.
- Use colors and color combinations carefully.
- Use windows to organize information.
- Use different type sizes / styles for emphasis and variety.
- Use graphics whenever possible.
- Use titles and headings on all screens if possible.
- Display resolution affects screen quality.

6/ User Control

A single design rule dictates the success of most software: the user should always be in control of the program. Software which fails to follow this rule will not usually be accepted by users. This chapter describes how to design programs which allow maximum user control.

When you design a program, imagine that you are designing the control panel of a car, airplane or nuclear reactor, i.e., something to be operated by someone. Your major concern should be what kind of controls to provide the user and how to lay out the control panel. If you do a good job, people will be able to use the program effortlessly and enjoyably. On the other hand, if you do a poor job, people will find the program frustrating and difficult to use.

One of the most important goals that every software designer should strive for is *transparency* . In a transparent program, the user completely forgets that they are interacting with a computer program and focuses totally on the task. Simulations and games frequently achieve transparency. In fact, if you want to see examples of complete transparency, visit a video game arcade sometime.

Pacing

One of the most common and serious mistakes made in the design of programs is to have the program set the pace for the user. For example, the rate at which words, sentences, or graphics are displayed may be paced or the length of time a screen is displayed is controlled by the program. Since everyone reads at a different speed, controlling the rate of display means that most people will be forced to read faster or more slowly than their natural rate. Furthermore, if they are distracted for a few seconds or minutes, they may miss information.

To avoid this problem, always allow users to set their own pace by selecting the next display or event. Having the user press a key to continue is a common method of doing this. Also, put text and graphics on the screen as quickly as possible. Create attention by other effects (e.g. different type styles or sizes, boxing, highlighting) rather than by pauses or display timing.

An exception to this rule is animation. In an animated sequence you will want to control the timing for a brief period. However, you should allow the user to start/stop the animation sequence so they feel some degree of control. Other exceptions include programs where timed presentation is important such as a speed reading program or certain events in a simulation/game.

In simulations and games, you may want to provide the user with a pause option. This allows the user to stop the action at any time and study the situation. Action is resumed when the pause is turned off.

Sequencing

In addition to control of pacing, the user should also control all aspects of sequencing. This includes both intra and inter unit sequencing. Within a unit, the user should have the capability to go back to a previous screen, question, or event (i.e., undo), to get help or advice, and to exit at any time to a menu or command level. The review capability is needed because people often want to check what they just saw or did. (Starting over again from the beginning of a unit is not an acceptable form of review!) The need for help at any time should be obvious. The capability to quit at any time allows people to interrupt the unit when they want to do something else.

Users should also be able to get to any part of the program from a main menu or command level. This means that users can decide the order in which they take units. Users should be able to go back through a seqence they have already completed and should not be locked out of any sequence.

A "resume" or "continue" option should be provided for when a user exits from a unit to go look at something else and then wants to return to the previous unit. This is especially important when a lot of work has been done in the unit which would be a lot of trouble to repeat. This option should also be available each time the user signs on to a previously started program. Expecting the user to remember where they left off is not good enough! The resume option is particularly handy after an accidental sign-off (e.g., when somebody trips over the power plug).

An exception to complete user control is the case of pre/post-tests, exams, or questionnaires which are used to assess the skill or knowledge level of a user. Since this information is needed by the program (or is used for grades or certification), it must be taken at a certain place in the program (e.g., right after sign-on) and must be completed in full. However, the user should still have the capability to back up and skip questions, as well as change answers.

Menus

There are basically four ways to allow users to control a program (other than direct answers to questions): menus, command languages, function keys and cursor movement. Menus consist of a list of options or selections. With a command language, special keywords or phrases are typed in. Function keys are additional keys provided on the keyboard that are assigned unique functions (e.g., help, next, exit) by the programmer. Function keys are usually labelled F1, F2, F3, etc. Cursor control allows users to select fields or move about the screen using arrow keys or some form of pointing input (e.g., touch, mouse, trackball).

Menus are usually better than command languages because they are quicker to learn, don't require memorizing keywords or parameters, and eliminate the possibility of syntax errors. However, experienced users of a program typically prefer command languages or function keys since they allow you to accomplish things faster. The best solution is to provide two types of control options (e.g., menus and function keys) to accomodate both new and experienced users.

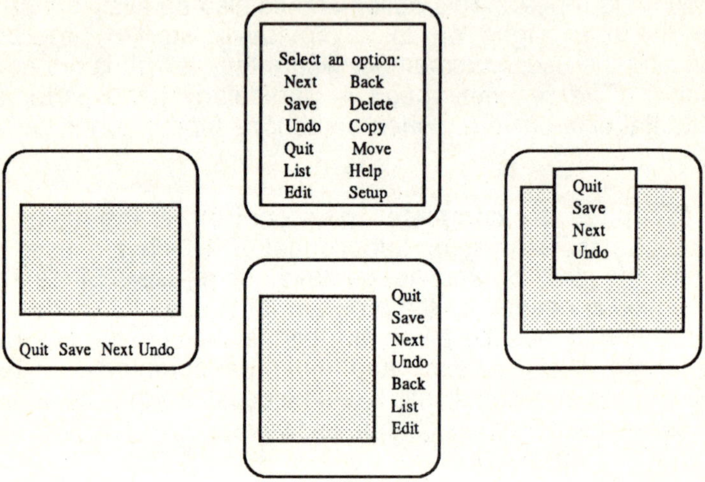

Menus can be at the top, bottom, side, full screen, or overlaid (pop-up).

Menus are used for two different purposes: to present control options and to provide choices among content selections. Any time there are three or more options or choices, some form of menu is warranted. Menus can come in a variety of formats. Content selections are typically full page menus that use a complete screen to list the alternatives. Control option menus usually consist of a list of options (words or icons) that are displayed along the top, bottom, or side of the screen. Pull-down menus use an overlapping window that appears when a keyword or icon is selected.

One of the major problems with menus is that they become cumbersome to move through once there are more than two or three levels. One way of overcoming this problem is to lay out different levels of menu options in a two line menu bar. Such a menu bar looks like this:

Option1 Option2 Option3 Option 4
Option1.1 Option1.2 Option1.3 Option1.4

When the cursor is on an option, the suboptions for that option (i.e., the next level of menu items) are displayed on the line underneath. Selection of an option causes all of the suboptions to replace the main options on the first line and the next level of options to appear on the second line. Using this technique, it is possible to quickly traverse through many levels of menus. To speed up the selection, the first letter of the option name can be entered instead of using the cursor to select options. A control key (such as Escape) is used to back up levels. A third line can be used to provide a brief description of the currently selected option.

For example, here is a typical menu bar for an editor:

Edit Load Save Print Exit
Insert Delete Copy Add Quit

In this example, the cursor is currently on the Edit option and the suboptions for Edit are shown on the second line. If Edit is selected (by pressing the Enter key or clicking a mouse), the menu bar would change to the following:

Insert Delete Copy Add Quit
Character Line Paragraph Page

With the cursor on Insert, the suboptions for Insert are identified on the second line. If Insert is selected, the menu bar changes as follows:

Character Line Paragraph Page
Place cursor before character to be inserted

With the Character option selected, the second line provides a prompt message. If this option is selected, the character insert function will be performed.

Function keys can be used in conjunction with menus by displaying the current function of each key along the bottom or side of the screen. This reminds the user what each function key does. It also provides a way to show when certain function keys are active/inactive or to redefine the function of a specific key in different parts of a program (not usually a good idea). Icons can be used for the same purpose as function keys and permit a greater range of choices.

The design of menu structures has been the subject of much human factors research. There are a number of considerations about the ordering of items in a menu or how to go from one level of menu to another and back. See the references to the human factors literature provided in Appendix B for further information.

User Customization

Almost every program has some aspect that users could change to suit their own needs, interests or preferences. This includes characteristics of the display (e.g., window sizes, number of lines/columns per screen), the difficulty level of the presentation, or the actual content presented. The more customization capability provided, the more useful the program will be to the user.

The most important kind of customization is the ability to replace the content of the program in terms of headings, examples, questions, and feedback messages. One of the typical problems with many application programs is that they can't be tailored to meet user needs or can't be updated easily. This problem is usually handled by only using the parts of the program that are relevant or up to date. However, if you provide the capability for the user to easily type in their own content, or modify content already there, this problem can be overcome. For example, in a reservation program, new options may be announced or some options may not be available for all customers. Users need to be able to make these changes. Any program that has to do with products or procedures should have customization capabilities since this type of information is always changing.

The ability to change difficulty levels is also a useful customization feature, especially for a program that will be used by people with a variety of different backgrounds and skill levels. However, to have this kind of customization, it is necessary to create material at different levels and to categorize the material created into different levels of difficulty. Generally, there will be three levels: the "normal" level of explanation appropriate for most users, a more detailed explanation for those who lack the background, and a "fast track" with a concise level of explanation (expert level). The major problem with difficulty levels is trying to identify good criteria to differentiate the categories.

One drawback to customization is that it allows each user to create a different version of the program which may be inconsistent with other versions of the program. In environments where standardization is important (e.g., systems that share a networked database), this can create a problem. The trick is to provide customization in such a way that it does not affect the function of the program. Another possiblity is to require some type of authorization (e.g., special password) to customize a program. This authorization can be given only to users who are properly trained to make changes.

Defaults

To make it easier and faster for users to respond, every option should have a default action. If the user does not make a new choice (i.e., simply presses the RETURN/ENTER key or clicks the mouse), the default action will be taken. Default actions should always be displayed so that the user knows what the default is. The default action should be the most common or the recommended (i.e., safest) choice for a response, the current file, or the last selection made. For example, the defaults which are highlighted in bold below represent the recommended, current and most common choices respectively:

DO YOU WISH TO SAVE BEFORE EXITING? **YES** NO
NAME OF FILE TO SAVE: **LESSON1**
TRANSMISSION SPEED: 300 **1200** 2400

One of the major advantages of defaults for new or casual users is that they can select the defaults without having to know what the other options mean initially.

In selections where the choices are arbitrary, make the first option the default as a convention.

Multiple (Redundant) Control Options

One of the difficulties in designing things for people is that they all have different preferences. The way to handle this with respect to program control is to provide multiple options that do the same thing. For example, options can be selected by moving the cursor or by a control key combination. If you wanted to quit, you could select the QUIT option on the menu or just press CONTROL Q. Alternatively, you could use function keys and menu options for the same functions or command words and menu options.

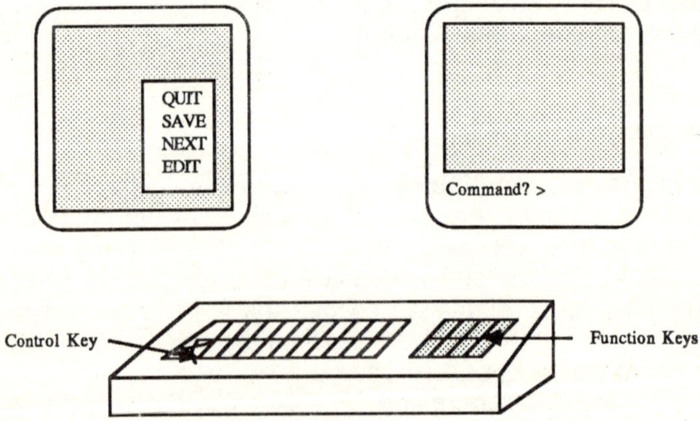

User control can be provided via menus, commands, control keys, and function keys.

When you design redundant control options, you should focus on the difference between novice and experienced computer users. Novice users will generally prefer menus while more experienced users will prefer control keys, function keys, and commands. Function keys are appropriate when you only need a small number (up to 10) of options. Control keys can be used to represent a large number of options (up to about 40). Commands are typically used when the options have parameters (e.g., SPEED 1200) or can be combined.

By the way, another good reason for redundant control options is to allow the program to continue to function in the event of an equipment problem. For example, if you have written a program that is totally dependent on a mouse or trackball for selecting options and this device breaks, the user is out of luck. However, if you have provided a redundant set of control options via control or function keys, the program can still be used. Most systems that use touch input provide an alternative input mode through the keyboard in case the touch input is disabled or loses its calibration. The same precaution should be taken with systems that use speech input/output.

Summary

Here are the guidelines for designing user control:

- Always let the user set the pace.
- Allow users to control sequencing.
- Use menus as much as possible.
- Let the user customize the program.
- Always provide defaults.
- Provide multiple (redundant) control options.

6/ User Control

7/ Response Processing

This chapter presents guidelines for giving directions, asking questions, checking input, and providing feedback. All of these activities are related to the analysis of user responses. The way that directions or questions are phrased can make a big difference in the kind of responses made. Input checking is the heart of response analysis. Feedback tells the user what happened to their response. As mentioned in Chapter 2, the kind of response analysis in a program determines the nature of the interactivity.

Figure 7-1 shows the major steps in response processing that are covered in this chapter. These steps will be required in any type of program and with any type of input.

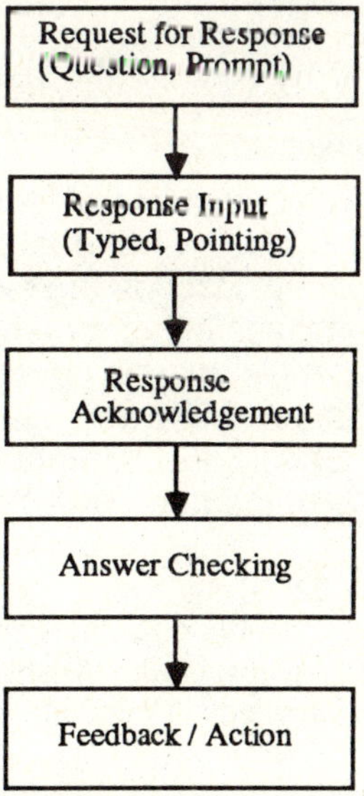

Figure 7-1

7/ Response Processing

Stating Directions and Questions Clearly

A lot of input checking effort (and user frustration) can be eliminated by careful wording of directions and questions. Directions and questions should be phrased so that the expected answer is clear-cut. Say exactly what you want the user to do. Wherever possible provide an example as part of the directions or question. For example, consider the following input requests:

> Enter the date:
> What is the customer's name?
> Do you know why Washington chopped down the cherry tree?

Each of these requests is ambiguous and is likely to lead to a variety of unexpected responses. Here are improved versions of these questions:

> Type the date (mm/dd/yy):
> Type the customer's name (first/last):
> Type a sentence which explains why Washington chopped down the cherry tree:

Notice the nature of the changes to the questions. First, they state exactly what the user is expected to do (i.e., type something). Secondly, they describe the expected format for the answer. However, even these improvements still contain quite a lot of ambiguity. For example, do you have to enter two numbers for month / day or will one do? Do you put slashes between the numbers or names? Should the sentence have punctuation? Here are better versions of the three questions:

> Type the date (e.g., 02/25/88):
> Type the customer's name (e.g., John Smith):
> Type a sentence that explains why Washington chopped down the cherry tree (punctuation not needed).

Making your directions or questions as clear as possible will not totally eliminate all potential mistakes or confusion, but it will sure help! If you find it very difficult to state the directions clearly, it may be a hint that the program (or the specific response required) is too complicated.

Many problems are created by making incorrect assumptions about what users know. For example, you instruct the user to press F1 for a certain function, meaning the function key F1. However, a new computer user may not know about function keys and presses the F and 1 keys instead, producing an error.

Pointing Responses Versus Typed Input

Design menus and questions so that the user selects an option via some form of pointing response (arrow keys, mouse, touch, etc.) rather than by typing something from the keyboard. This eliminates the need for error checking and allows the user to respond faster. Any type of computer can be programmed for some type of pointing response. For example, the space bar can be used to move across the options and the ENTER/RETURN key pressed to select something. Almost all keyboards in use today have arrow keys, and a mouse is becoming increasingly common.

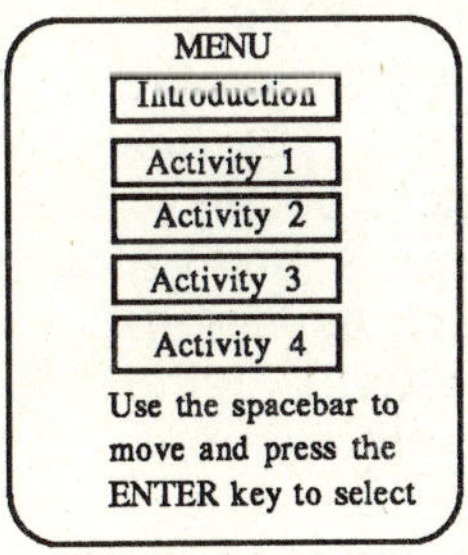

This...

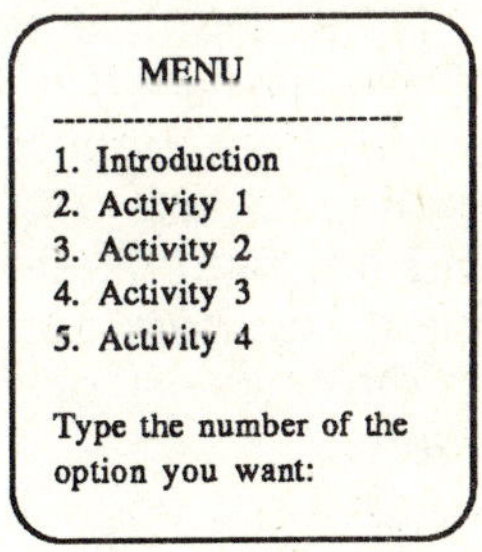

...Not This.

Clearly, questions that require text or numerical input or that involve a recall rather than recognition type answer will require the use of the keyboard. Actually, it is possible to do this by pointing too, since numbers or letters can be displayed on the screen and selected one at a time. Most arcade games (which lack keyboards) use this method for entry of names or numerical information.

Acknowledging User Input

Programs should provide a response for every user input, even if it is just an acknowledgement such as "ok" or "wait". Users need to know that their input has been recognized by the program. Normally, a response will result in an immediate feedback message or change in the display. When the response may take more than a few seconds (e.g., complex calculations in a simulation or a search in a large database), a "wait" message should be displayed from the time the input is made until the response is provided.

Exceptions to the need for acknowledgement are data entry displays involving multiple fields. Advancing to the next field is usually sufficient acknowledgment of input.

Response Variations

With typed input, it is necessary to check for variations in responses provided. For example, your program should ignore the case (i.e., upper/lower) of the response unless this is relevant to the answer. Blank spaces before or after the answer should not matter either. It's also a good idea to check for common keyboard confusions such as typing O for 0 (i.e., the letter O for zero) or I for 1 (i.e., the letter I for one) and vice-versa.

Some authoring system programs designed for creating instructional programs allow you to set a spelling tolerance for answer matching. If the answer contains only one or two incorrect letters, the response is judged as an acceptable match. In addition, you can usually specify exactly what part of an answer is important and must be in the response using some type of delimiter. The parts of the answer that are irrelevant can be indicated by using "wild card" characters.

For example, suppose that you were interested in matching the specific phrase: "computers are wonderful". You could specify this in the following form: %c*mput*rs*are*w*nderful*%, where the % signs specify the exact string to be matched and the * denotes positions in the answer where any character is acceptable ("wild cards"). The following answers would be acceptable matches according to this specification:

computors are wonderfull
cumputers are wunderful
computersare wonderful

The following phrases, however, would not match this specification:

computer are wonderful
computers are wonderous
computers are not wonderful

Of course, the answer specification could be changed to allow a widor range of alternatives if desired. This is up to the program designer.

One of the major frontiers in the design of user interfaces is natural language and speech input. Most people would prefer to interact with a computer by typing or speaking in regular English (or whatever language) sentences and phrases. Clearly this would allow programs to be much more tolerant of variations in user responses. On the other hand, a tremendous amount of knowledge is required by the program to understand what the user means. This knowledge must be provided by the designer and involves a great deal of work, far beyond the current levels of effort normally associated with developing software.

Research in the areas of artificial intelligence and expert systems is concerned with how to design and develop such natural language and speech recognition capabilities (see references in Appendix B). It is reasonable to expect that these modes of response will become more common as more progress is made in these areas.

7/ Response Processing

> Natural language understanding and speech recognition capability are now widely available and in use with many types of programs and machines (including personal computers). However, these capabilities are still fairly limited in terms of the size of the vocabulary they can handle (typically only a few hundred words). With speech recognition, there is the additional problem of accents and idiosyncratic pronunciation. Current capabilities are acceptable for a number of applications; however, further advances in the field of artificial intelligence are needed for this to be a routine feature of programs.

Changing Answers

One thing to keep in mind when designing response processing sequences is that people frequently make inadvertant choices or change their mind about answers they have made. For this reason, users should be able to change their answers or selections before they are processed. This is especially true of responses which have important consequences, such as:

- deleting a file or data records
- saving something with a name that already exists (i.e., replacement)
- exiting from a program without saving current work
- any data entered that will be used often in the program (e.g., names, dates, times, addresses)

Before one of these actions is processed by the program, the user should be asked for a confirmation:

Are you sure you want to delete the file _____? OK CANCEL
The mailing address is _______ CORRECT INCORRECT

The general technique is to redisplay the specific action requested or data entered and ask if this is correct. If the user indicates that it is not correct, they are returned to the previous menu or the question so that they can correct the response or do something else.

7/ Response Processing

Responses should always require a separate keypress (i.e., the ENTER/ RETURN key) to allow the user to make corrections before the response is processed. With typed input, the user can use the backspace key to change their answer before pressing ENTER/RETURN. With a pointing response, they can select another option before entering. Response analysis in which the answer is processed as soon as a certain number of characters are typed, or as soon as an option is selected, does not give users a chance to change their mind or correct errors and is poorly designed.

The ability to change answers is particularly important in completing online forms, tests or surveys. In the paper versions, people have the capability to review questions and change their answers if they want. It is important to provide the same type of capability in a computerized version. This means that users should be able to go back and look at previous questions, see the answers they picked and change the answers. This capability should be available at any time, not just at the end.

In terms of program design, this review and "rub-out" capability means that your program will need to have BACK and NEXT options to allow users to get to the question they want to review and you will need to display their current answer. If the questions are randomly selected or generated, you will need to store them so they can be re-displayed in the original order.

When the user goes back to a question that was previously answered, the cursor should be located on the last character of a typed answer (so they can backspace to erase it) or on the previously selected option in a pointing type response. If the user decides not to change their previous answer, their current response or option selected stays the same when they press ENTER / RETURN.

Providing Corrective Feedback

When the user makes an error or types an incorrect answer to a question, the feedback message should suggest the correct format for the answer. Avoid messages that tell users they made an "error" or that they were "wrong". For example:

> Type in the date (mm/dd/yy): 31/5/86
> *** ERROR 069: Field exceeds acceptable range ***

Not only is this type of error message intimidating, it is also not very helpful in explaining what the error is. A better error message would be:

> The number you have entered for the month is too large.
> Type the month first, then the day and year.

This error message makes it clear what the problem is and doesn't affront the user. An even better error message would be:

> Do you mean 5/31/86? YES NO

This message allows the user to make the correction without having to retype the date. In order to have this type of error message, it is necessary to know (or guess) what kinds of errors are likely to be made.

Incidentally, this particular example points out some of the difficulties in developing programs for international use. In Canada and Europe, dates are usually in the form: dd/mm/yy. This adds an additional element of confusion for entering dates. It also emphasizes why it is so important to provide an example of the format expected for a data entry field.

Nature of Feedback Messages

Feedback messages should be brief (e.g., one or two words whenever possible). When the response is incorrect or inappropriate, an explanation of why should be provided (or the user should be directed towards HELP for a full explanation).

Some designers feel that it is important to provide variety in feedback messages. Instead of using the same "Correct" or "Ok" message for each answer, they prefer to randomly generate a different message each time (e.g., "Right", "Good", "That's it.", etc.) from a stored list. There is no evidence to suggest that this is very important to users. In fact, different messages each time may slow down users because they must take extra time to recognize them.

Sarcasm or any sort of demeaning feedback messages should be avoided. Humor in feedback messages should also be avoided in most circumstances. The problem with using humor is that its effectiveness varies tremendously across individuals. What some people find funny, others will find offensive or puzzling. Unless you are sure that the humor will work for all users, you should skip it.

Summary

Here are the guidelines for response processing presented in this chapter:

- State directions and questions so that errors are unlikely
- Use pointing rather than typed input whenever possible.
- Always acknowledge user input in some way.
- Answer analysis should be tolerant of variations in response.
- Allow users to change their answers.
- Always provide corrective feedback for errors or wrong answers.
- Feedback should be brief and neutral in tone.

7/ Response Processing

8/ Helps

A great deal of thought needs to go into how to make programs as usable as possible. Helps represent one of the more powerful and unobtrusive ways of making a program more usable. They are powerful because they can provide very specific information exactly when it is needed. They are unobtrusive because the information is hidden until the user requests it.

Helps are a form of embedded training, i.e., instruction which is an integral part of a computer-based system or product. Embedded training can be built into any type of automated office or manufacturing system, computer-controlled equipment (such as aircraft, appliances, "smart" weapons, etc.), and any type of computer system (e.g., administrative, banking, inventory, retail sales). As more and more systems and products become computer-based, embedded training in the form of helps and advisors will become increasingly common.

There are a number of different types of helps (see Table 8-1). *Fixed Format* (or context independent) helps produce the same information regardless of what the user has done. The most familiar kind of fixed format help is an explanation of a command. Online reference manuals or job aids are also common examples of fixed format helps. Fixed format helps are the simplest type of help to implement since they only involve the creation of text files.

Table 8-1

Types of Helps
1. Fixed Format
2. Context-Sensitive
3. Prompting
4. Query-in-depth
5. Dialog (Conversational)
6. Adaptive

In contrast, *Context-Sensitive* helps provide information that depends upon what the user is currently trying to do. For example, if you were in the middle of a spreadsheet creating a formula and you asked for help, you would get information about creating formulas. Later, if you were editing the same formula and you asked for help, you would get information about editing formulas. With a context-sensitive help, the program attempts to provide information specific to your current activity.

Prompting type helps are similar to context-sensitive helps except that they are generated by the system rather than being requested by the user. For example, if a user types a command in the wrong format or with the wrong parameters, a prompting help system will automatically display the correct format of the command. A sophisticated help system will actually attempt to correct the mistake and display the corrected command to the user for verification (i.e., "Did you mean....").

Query-in-depth helps provide multiple levels of information. Each successive help request provides more elaboration or detail than the previous level. Thus, if you ask for an explanation of a particular command, the first help may simply provide the purpose and correct format. A second request for help may provide examples of use or a full description of how and when the command can be used. A third request may produce the full documentation on the command from the reference manual. These different levels of help may be accessed by successive help requests or the level may be set as a parameter of the program. A common way of implementing query-in-depth is to put increasingly more detailed information in successive help screens and allow the user to return to the application after each help screen or continue with more helps.

Dialog type helps allow the user to ask questions in a conversational format. Such helps depend upon some form of natural language understanding capability to work. Users type their question in natural language. The following is an example of a dialog type help sequence:

USER: How do I copy all my files to a new diskette?
HELP: Use the command, copy a:*.* b:
USER: What are a: and b: ?

HELP:	a: refers to the left drive and b: refers to the right drive
USER:	I still don't understand what to do.
HELP:	To make a complete copy of a diskette, put the source diskette in the left drive and the new diskette in the right drive, then type the command, copy a:*.* b: and press ENTER.
USER:	Ok, thanks.
HELP:	You're welcome.

Needless to say, there are only a few systems available today capable of this advanced type of help (see the article by Wilensky et al. about the UNIX Consultant in Appendix B).

The last type of help to be mentioned is *Adaptive* helps. An adaptive help keeps track of how much the user knows about the system and adjusts the level of help information provided accordingly. Thus, a request for help at a particular place will produce different information when the user is new than when the user has used the system for a while. Alternatively, the help system may limit the actual functions available to the user until certain basic operations have been mastered. To have an adaptive help capability, it is usually necessary for the program to build a user model that represents what the user currently knows about the system. The user model is used to make decisions about what kind of help to present to the user.

Making Helps Specific

In order to be helpful, helps must provide the specific information needed by the user. Table 8-2 lists some typical categories of

Table 8-2

Categories Of Helps That May Be Needed

1. Information about current location or status
2. Description of current options
3. Explanation of what things do (e.g. commands)
4. Description of format for input
5. Explanation of error messages/conditions
6. Explanation of output displays
7. Information about how the program works
8. Explanation of terms (glossary)

information that users may need help with. To be comprehensive, a help system would provide this kind of information for every function and operation in a program.

In a fixed format type of help, there should be a help associated with every command or option. In a context-sensitive help system, there should be a help associated with every response sequence. One way of identifying all possible helps needed is to construct a matrix with functions or operations down the side and sequences or units across the top (see Figure 8-3). Each cell in the matrix is a potential help.

	Unit1	Unit2	Unit3	Unit4	Unit5
Add	X			X	
Copy			X		X
Delete	X				X
Rename			X	X	
Replace		X	X		X
Exit	X			X	X

Figure 8-3

Different Helps for Different Users

Because of differences in background experiences and interests, different types of helps will be needed for different types of users. One dimension of difference is computer experience. Users who have little experience with computers will need help with very basic things such as being reminded to press the ENTER/RETURN key after selecting a response or putting diskettes in a disk drive correctly. On the other hand, experienced computer users will need more sophisticated help having to do with shortcuts and limitations. One of the ironies about these two groups of users is that they are both likely to be very impatient and intolerant of the computer -- but for quite different reasons. The novice doesn't want to learn any more than necessary to use the machine; the expert wants to learn how to do things as quickly and efficiently as possible.

8/ Helps

Research shows that inexperienced computer users are often overwhelmed and confused by help systems. This suggests that help systems intended for novices should be either fairly simple (i.e., fixed format) or very sophisticated (i.e., prompting or dialog). Help systems designed for novices should not add more complexity to the use of the system!

Users also differ in terms of their reasons for using a computer. Some people will need to use a computer system infrequently (e.g., to perform annual inventories, generate monthly reports, or update customer records). Other people will use a computer system on a routine basis for most of their work (e.g., bank tellers, reservation clerks, travel agents). Casual users will likely need different types of helps than frequent users.

The best way to determine what types of helps are needed by different groups of users is to observe their use of the system and identify the problems they have. Listings of their online sessions can be analyzed to identify the kinds of errors made and helps can be developed for these errors. Once the helps are implemented, the analysis process is repeated to see how well the helps work and what new problems arise. Note that this is a general methodology for designing helps; it is not just for discovering the differences between different user groups.

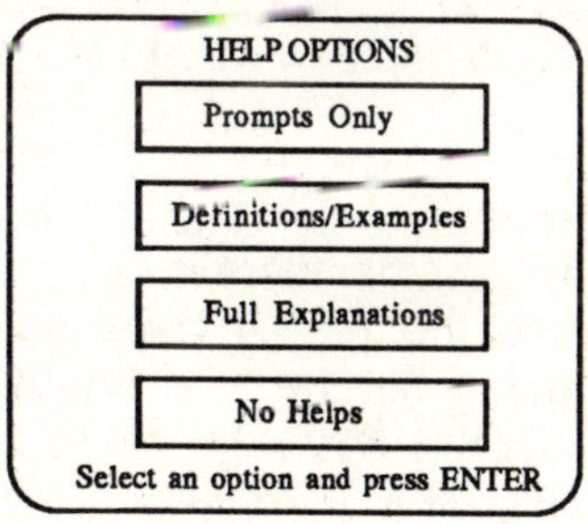

Allow users to specify the level of help.

Incidentally, a major problem with identifying helps for different types of users is that users tend to change categories. A novice computer user can quickly become an experienced user after using the system a few times. Casual users may become frequent users and vice-versa. It is a good idea to allow users to set the kind or level of help provided so they can tailor it to their current level and needs. This can be done by providing a menu that allows the user to set the help options (or turn help off completely if desired).

The default setting for the help options should be full explanations rather than no helps. The program instructions should tell the user about the ability to change the help options. If there is a help for help, it should also explain how to change help levels.

Availability and Accessibility

It seems relatively obvious that if helps are to be useful they must be available whenever needed and they must be easy to get to. However, helps are frequently not provided for all functions/operations in a program and they are sometimes "hidden" from the user. It is critical that helps be complete and easy to access.

If helps are only available at certain times or places in a program, there should be some kind of indication of when help is available. This is usually done by displaying the word "help" or a help icon somewhere on the screen when help is active.

Helps can be activated via a fixed or function key, a typed command, or selection of an option that is always displayed on the screen. On some keyboards, there is a key labelled "Help". It is also common to use the F1 function key for help. The standard typed command for help is the word "help" or a question mark. Usually, it is also possible to type specific help commands such as "help print" or "? save". With keys or typed commands, it is necessary to remind the user that help is available. With a continuously displayed help option, the user is always aware of its availability.

It is important to design helps so that they do not disrupt the work flow of the user. Helps must always return the user to the point in the program where they left off to get help. It is highly desirable to provide help information in a pop-up window that overlays the current application. When the user is finished with the help, the window should disappear. If a window can't be used and new displays are required for the help, the original application display should be recreated when the user returns from the help. Helps which cause the original application to scroll off the screen make it difficult for users to remember where they left off (and sometimes what their exact problem was).

Accuracy and Completeness

The information provided by helps must be correct and complete otherwise the user's trust and confidence in the system will be undermined. If the helps explain that a function works one way and the user finds that it actually works differently, the user is not likely to believe any other help information provided (even if it is accurate). Quality review methods (see Chapter 10) are especially important for helps.

A common reason why helps are inaccurate or contain omissions is because changes have been made to the system or product but the helps have not been updated. To prevent this problem, it is critical to establish development procedures which require help information to be changed at the same time as the application functions. This is accomplished most easily if the help functions are considered to be a major part of the application and hence have the same revision priority as any other part of the system.

One important kind of information often missing from helps is examples. Examples provide concrete illustrations and are sometimes the easiest type of help information to understand. Examples should cover typical situations as well as counter-examples and anomalies. For example:

```
>help print
.The PRINT command prints out all or part of a document or file.
.It has the format PRINT [Starting page] [Ending page]
.Examples:
    PRINT 1,20    prints pages 1 to 20 inclusive
    PRINT 10      prints page 10
    PRINT 10,     prints all pages starting with page 10
    PRINT ,20     prints pages 1 to 20 inclusive (same as PRINT 1,20)
```

PRINT prints all pages
PRINT -1,20 prints pages 1 to 20 inclusive
Note that negative numbers and zero are treated as 1

In a context-sensitive type of help system, it is possible to tailor the examples to the user's current situation. For example, if the user is currently using a certain file, the help may insert this file name in the examples used.

The help information provided to the user is sometimes incomplete because the user did not request all of the information available. For example, a user might set the help level to definitions only but the information needed for a specific problem might only be provided in the full explanation mode. This problem can be minimized if the description of the help system (i.e., help help) explains what kind of information is provided by different levels of help or different types of help requests. It is also a good idea to provide an index and cross-reference for helps accessed from a help submenu. In addition, helps that only provide partial information should indicate that further information is available and how to access it (e.g., "Press help again to see examples or ENTER to continue with the program").

Summary

Here are the guidelines presented in this chapter for the design of helps:

- Make helps as specific as possible.
- Different types of helps are needed for different users.
- Helps should always be available and easy to access.
- Ensure that help information is accurate and complete.

9/ Troubleshooting

Troubleshooting involves finding the existing and potential problems in a program. This includes finding and correcting the errors in your program as well as dealing with errors made by users when using the program. This chapter discusses both types of troubleshooting. The handling of errors is a very important aspect of the design process and a characteristic that distinquishes well designed programs from poorly designed ones.

A number of design factors affect the likelihood of errors in programs. If a programming system (see Chapter 1) is used to create the program, the program should be relatively free of "bugs". If user responses are always made via menus (as recommended in Chapter 6), the kinds of errors possible are reduced considerably. If directions and questions are stated clearly (as discussed in Chapter 7), the chances of an incorrect response being made are lessened.

The way the program is designed and implemented can also affect the likelihood of errors. Programs should be designed, developed, and tested in small pieces or *modules.* Errors in a program are much easier to find and fix if modules are created and tested individually and then combined. A program is also easier to revise if it is divided into modules. Only the modules that need revision are changed; the others can be left alone. In addition, modularization also increases user control since it alllows the user to move about the program easier (assuming the modules are accessible).

Testing for Both Expected and Unexpected Responses

There are basically two kinds of user answers you need to check for: expected responses and unexpected responses. Expected responses are the answers that a user would make if they were responding as you anticipated. This includes data input fields, correct and incorrect answers to questions or problems and selection of options in a menu. Unexpected responses are responses that a user shouldn't make. This includes pressing special keys (e.g., Escape, Backspace, Tab) or unusual combinations of keys, entering text when numbers should be entered (or vice-versa), entering numbers out of range or text that is too long, pointing to things outside of the current response area and incorrect punctuation in responses.

Keep in mind that most of these unexpected responses are accidental, not deliberate. This is why they are usually nonsensical and difficult to anticipate. For example, a user meant to press the shift key to type a capital "C" but instead pressed the control key and entered control "C". In many programs, control "C" is a command used to interrupt processing. Suppose that a user presses the F1 key (a function key) when they meant to just press the "1" key. If the function keys are used for user control options, the response will be different than expected. In many cases, overanxious users press the ENTER/RETURN key before they have typed their response. This results in a blank response.

As a specific example, consider the error handling required for the spreadsheet example discussed in Chapter 2. The spreadsheet allows three types of input: function keys, arrow keys to move the cursor, and cell entries. Here are some of the possible input errors that would need to be checked:

- Invalid function key (i.e., not currently defined)
- Attempt to move the cursor into an undefined area (e.g., off the screen)
- Invalid cell entry (unrecognized symbol, improper syntax for formula)
- Invalid keypresses (e.g., Control, Escape, Tab)

Bullet-Proofing

To properly test your program for errors, you need to try every possible input response for every possible input sequence. This exhaustive testing of all possibilities is called *bullet-proofing*. A program that has been completely bullet-proofed can handle any response, no matter how bizarre (including turning off the machine). The program should respond to an unexpected response by prompting for the desired response or option(s).

Bullet-proofing is not as difficult as it may sound, although it can be very tedious and time-consuming. Most input sequences can be programmed so that any reponse other than the expected ones are directed to the same error message. Once this error handling routine has been thoroughly checked, it can be used throughout the program with the knowledge that it will work for every input sequence it is included in. Bullet-proofing then reduces to checking that the routine has been correctly placed in every input sequence.

Bullet-proofing typed input is much more difficult than bullet-proofing menu selections. You have to worry about punctuation, upper/lower case, word order, blank spaces, incorrect symbols (e.g., +\=/-&"), not to mention the content of the answer. Even something as simple as a numerical answer can lead to problems with commas and decimal places (e.g., compare 1000.0 versus 1,000 versus 1,000.00).

The real dilemma with bullet-proofing is that there is no way to know for sure that your program will catch all errors. Until the day when somebody discovers a reliable technique for proving the correctness of a program, it is all a matter of trial and error. The more trials, the fewer errors.

Checking the Range of Answers

One simple but highly useful error handling technique is range checking. This means checking the user's response to see if it is within an acceptable range for the answer. In the case of a numerical response, the number entered could be too small or too large. For example, if you asked the user to enter heart rate in a medical diagnostic program, the correct range would be 0-200. Any number outside of that range would produce a message such as "The number you entered is too high (low), please re-enter."

With text answers, the appropriate range to check is the number of characters or words anticipated. Thus if the correct answer is a 10 letter word or a phrase consisting of 3 words, any answer which has more than 10 letters or 3 words is incorrect. Note that a few extra characters or words should be allowed for since the user may add spaces or articles (i.e., the, a).

A more sophisticated type of range checking is made possible by using the artificial intelligence technique of "frames". A frame is a procedure or set of concepts that defines the relationships appropriate for a specific context. The frame has "slots" for things that belong in that context. For example, a frame for calculating a budget would include slots for all the appropriate cost components and their dependencies. When one number is entered, the frame would expect other numbers to be entered that are associated with it. Using a frame, it is possible to check for input which is missing or information which is inappropriate.

Drawing Attention to Errors

Error messages are often not noticed by users because the error message doesn't attract their attention. For example, an error message may be displayed at the bottom or top of the screen and then disappear when any key is pressed. The user may press a key before ever seeing the message. The worst kind of error messages are those that simply flash on the screen for a few seconds and are then erased immediately. If the user looks away during this instant (perhaps to look something up in a manual), they never see the message.

Error messages should catch the user's attention by being displayed in a separate window and require the user to make some sort of response. For example, an attempt to load or delete a file that doesn't exist should produce a message like:

File do.dat does not exist. Press ENTER to continue.

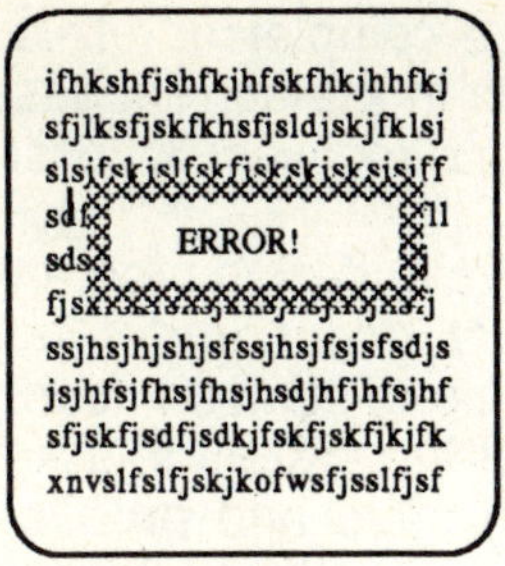

This...

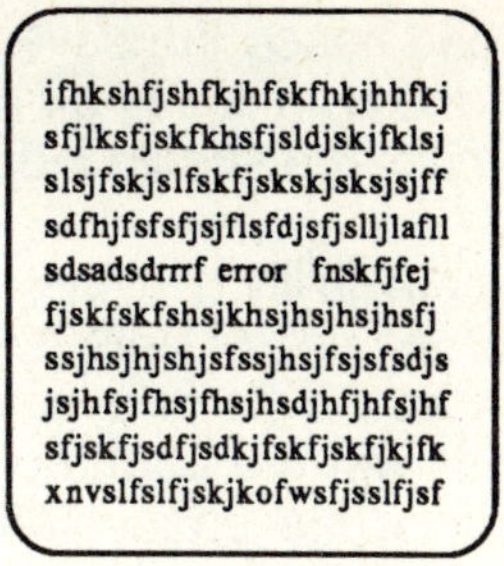

...Not This.

Error messages which are fairly serious in nature should be accompanied by a tone. For example, an attempt to save a a file that already exists or a disk full error should produce an auditory warning.

Explaining How to Correct A Problem

There is nothing more frustrating to a user than to receive an error message and have no idea what to do next. An error message should clearly state the nature of the problem (in English, not Computerese) and how to recover from the error. For example:

DISK DRIVE NOT READY   ABORT, IGNORE, RETRY ? >

is a standard error message received on a personal computer when you type a command that involves reading a diskette. What does this message mean and what are the recovery options? Typically this error message means that the latch on the disk drive is not closed. The recovery options are cancel (ABORT), continue (IGNORE) or repeat (RETRY) the command. A clearer version of this message would be:

Close latch on disk drive door. Type: CONTINUE, REPEAT, or CANCEL >

In some cases, there may be no recovery action possible for an error. One of the most notorious such errors is when a user tries to save a file and there is no space left on the disk. With some programs and systems, it is not possible to insert another disk at this point and hence the save cannot be completed. This may mean that the user loses all work done in the current session. The error message should indicate that no recovery is possible.

It is the responsibility of system designers to design programs so that "fatal" errors of this type do not occur under normal circumstances. This is a good example of how an "ounce of prevention is worth a pound of cure". If the system checked on the amount of file space left at each save and produced a warning message when it goe below a certain limit, this type of problem might be avoided. Similar kinds of preventative thinking can reduce the likelihood of major errors.

Retrys

Any reponse sequence that results in an error should allow the user to repeat or retry the response. For example, Figure 9-1

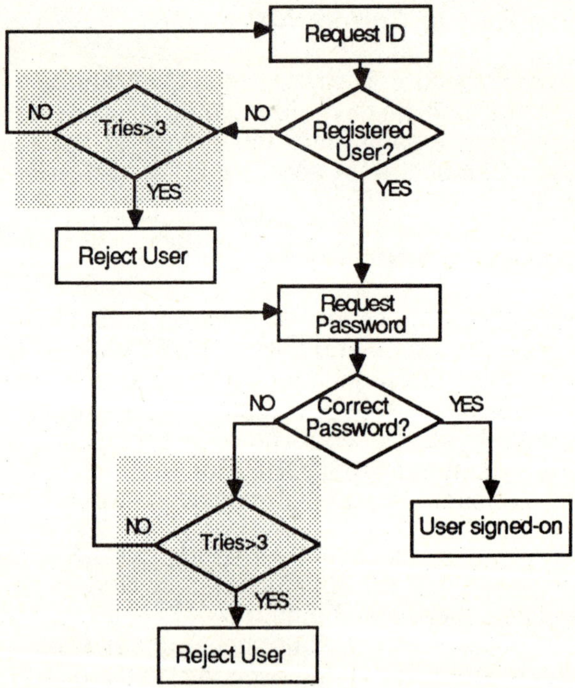

Figure 7-2

shows the sign-on sequence used in Chapter 2 with retry capabilities added to the response processing (shaded decision boxes) for both the id and password. This additional logic allows the user to try three times before the sign-on attempt is rejected. This retry capability is especially important in a sign-on sequence because users often forget their ids or passwords.

Recovering from Errors

When an unexpected response causes the program to fail, the program should allow the user to continue, resume or restart with minimal disruption and loss of work. Failing in a way that allows the user to recover is called "failing soft" as opposed to a "hard" failure which leaves the user helpless. For example, consider the most insidious of all computer failures: you accidently pull out the plug or the power fails. A good program will allow you to reconstruct what you were doing before the power went out.

Problems with disk drives or printers not being ready are a common source of program failures. For example, in any program that uses a printer, it is safe to assume that at some point the user will attempt to print something out and forget to turn the printer on. Unless this error has been taken into account, the user may get an obscure error message such as:

NOT READY ERROR WRITING DEVICE PRN

Instead, the program should detect that the printer is not turned on and provide a message such as: "The printer is not turned on, Please Correct and Press Enter."

Designing a program with good error recovery involves a lot of thought about what kind of problems might arise and how to deal with them. It also involves keeping track of what the user is doing so that if something goes wrong, the last state can be reconstructed. The difficult part about designing error recovery procedures is that you do not know why, how or when the program will fail (since it is likely to be caused by a bug or problem you can't anticipate).

A powerful UNDO function which "undoes" the most recent action is probably the best single "fail soft" capability. It allows the user to recover from any type of mistake and doesn't require the program designer to anticipate specific problems. Indeed, an UNDO function should be considered an essential component of any interactive program.

Usability Testing

A relatively new and important dimension of software development is the concept of usability testing, i.e., having users try out software (and associated documentation) to find out how well it works. A number of different types of testing can be conducted including:

- functional - does the program work as described in the documentation or specifications?
- performance - does the program work as well as expected or advertised?
- stress - how does the program behave when deliberately subjected to errors?
- compatability - does the program run properly on different machines or with other software?
- acceptance - does the program work well enough to be used or bought?

Different kinds of data collection techniques are used for different types of testing goals. Data may be collected by observation sessions and taped interviews, by questionnaires and surveys, or by online recording of responses and keystrokes. The data collected may be objective measures (such as the number of errors made or the time required to perform a task) or subjective information (such as preferences or attitudes). Occasionally, studies may be conducted that compare different versions of a program or documentation in terms of usability.

For a variety of reasons, it is highly desirable to have an independent group test your software. It ensures that the testing gets done thoroughly and eliminates a tedious development step for you. There are a number of companies and organizations that will test and certify your software. Two of the best known are the *International Bureau of Software Test* with major offices in Sunnyvale, CA, Marlboro, MA, and Round Rock, TX and the *Usability Test Laboratory of the American Institutes for Research* based in Washington, DC.

Summary

Here are the guidelines for troubleshooting:

- Test a program for both expected and unexpected responses.
- Check the range of answers.
- Draw the user's attention to the error.
- Tell the user how to correct the problem.
- Allow the user to retry.
- Always "fail soft" if possible.
- Include an UNDO function.

9/ Troubleshooting

10/ Quality Review

An important phase of development takes place after the initial program has been completed. This is the process of quality review and revision based upon the results of pilot or usability testing and actual use. In fact, the quality of much software comes from the changes made in the revision process, not the original version. It is essential to think of revision as a routine part of development activity, not something that is done just to "fix up" the program. Design is an iterative rather than linear process and involves continual changes.

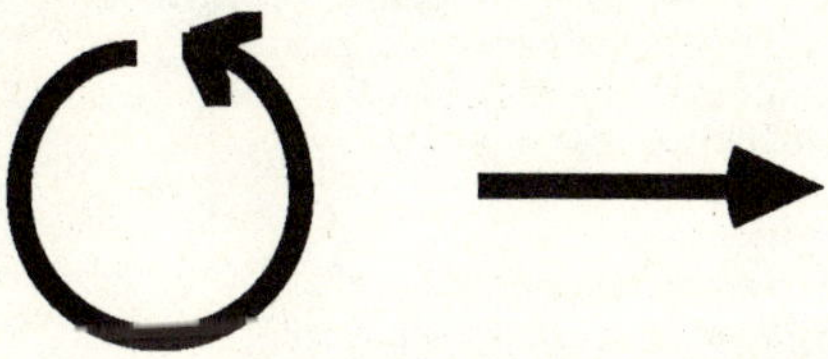

Design is an iterative, not linear, process.

When making revisions, changes should be based upon data and design guidelines rather than your own personal preferences. Everyone will have a slightly different opinion about how a screen should be organized or how a question should be phrased. Trying to keep everyone happy will drive you nuts! On the other hand, if different people make the same suggestions, then you should probably make the changes.

Systematic Review of Program Quality

An important step in developing high quality software is a systematic review that checks each unit or sequence in the program for design flaws. A checklist is very helpful for this purpose. Table 10-1 provides an example of a quality review

10/ Quality Review

Table 10-1

Quality Review Checklist

1. Content
   - Is the purpose of the program stated?
   - Is the sequence appropriate?
   - Is the level correct?
   - Is the information accurate and complete?

2. Language
   - Is the reading level too high?
   - Is the language free of bias?
   - Is the language free of jargon, slang, and idioms?
   - Is the spelling, grammar and punctuation correct?

3. Displays
   - Are the screens too crowded?
   - Are scrolling and overlays avoided?
   - Are windows used to organize information?
   - Are graphics used whenever possible?
   - Are different type styles / sizes used?
   - Are titles and headings used?

4. User Control
   - Does the user control the pace?
   - Can the user control the sequence?
   - Are menus used as much as possible?
   - Can users customize the program?
   - Are there multiple control options?
   - Are defaults provided?

5. Response Analysis
   - Are directions and questions stated clearly?
   - Is pointing input used wherever possible?
   - Is user input always acknowledged?
   - Does answer analysis tolerate response variation?
   - Can users change their answers easily?
   - Is corrective feedback provided?
   - Are feedback messages brief and neutral?

6. Helps
   - Are helps as specific as possible?
   - Are different levels of helps provided?
   - Are helps always available and easy to access?
   - Is help information accurate and complete?

checklist. It covers the guidelines discussed in the previous chapters plus considerations for content and language.

Since the content and language considerations are new, a few words of explanation are in order. Content considerations include purpose, level, sequence, accuracy, and completeness. The purpose of a program should be stated in an introduction (unless this is stated in ancillary materials). The sequencing of the program should take into account prerequisites among acitivities (e.g., making all necessary entries before running a balance). The level of the content should be appropriate for the users the program is designed for. The content should be accurate and complete.

Language considerations include reading level, bias, use of slang expressions or computer jargon, spelling, grammar and punctuation. Reading level represents the major factor determining how easy or hard it is to comprehend the text of your program. One of the interesting findings about reading level is that a lower reading level is better for everybody. (Better readers just read faster.) In fact, text written at a 5th grade reading level appears to be best for most users. A conversational style is generally recommended.

There are many kinds of bias that can creep into langauge. This includes cultural, sexual and racial bias. If you have ever used materials developed by someone in another country, you will probably have noticed cultural bias-- unfamiliar expressions, different forms of spelling, etc. Sexual bias refers to making assumptions about the sex of a person based upon role stereotypes (e.g., doctors are always male; nurses are always female) and the constant use of male referents (e.g., he, his, salesman). In a society that is committed to sexual equality, this type of bias in language is unacceptable. The same remarks hold for any sort of racial bias.

The avoidance of any sort of jargon, slang or idioms is important. The use of such terms or expressions introduces cultural bias and limits the number of people who will understand what is being said. Furthermore, it tends to date your program. So, be hip and cool it on the buzzwords, you dig?

Finally, you need to check spelling, grammar, and punctuation. While these kinds of mistakes are a relatively small matter, they can be distracting to the user. They also give the impression of carelessness or inaccuracy. This can undermine the credibility of the subject matter and the program.

The other considerations in the checklist have been discussed in previous chapters.

Using Response Data to Find Program Flaws

One of the ways in which revision of interactive software differs from traditional materials is the availability of detailed response data. This was touched upon briefly in Chapter 3. Every time the user makes a response, the nature of the response can be recorded. The response data collected can be used to evaluate user performance and to evaluate the effectiveness of the program. It is the latter purpose that is of interest for revision.

A standard way of examining response data is to look at a frequency table that shows the response of each user to every question, option or input request of the program. Figure 10-2 shows an example of this kind of frequency table. Each row represents a different user and each column represents a unique response. The entries indicate different types of responses (1 for correct response, 0 for incorrect, ? for help request, and blank for skipped). The row totals indicate the number of correct responses the user got across all questions; the column totals indicate the number of times each question was answered correctly.

Of course, it would be possible to total each type of response if desired (i.e., number of correct, incorrect, helps or skipped). Instead of correct answers to questions, we could be tabulating the number of times different options were selected or functions were used. The decision about what specific response data to collect depends upon what user records will be needed or what kinds of errors are anticipated.

Question Number

User	Q1	Q2	Q3	Q4	Q5	Q6	Total
U1	0	0	0	1	0		1
U2	1	0	?	1	1	0	3
U3	0	?	?	?	?	?	0
U4	1	1	1				3
U5	1	0	1	1	1	1	5
U6	1		0	1	0	1	3
U7	0	0	1	1	1	0	3
U8	?	?	1	1	0	1	3
Total	4	1	4	6	3	3	21

Figure 10-2

The data provided by Figure 10-2 suggests some possible problems with the program. For example, only one user answered question 2 correctly. This suggests that there is a problem with the presentation of information the question is associated with, or that the question is poorly worded, or that the question is too difficult for most users

Note that the table also gives us some insight into the behavior of certain users. User 3 avoided answering all of the questions after the first one by using help. The sequence may have been too difficult for this user. User 4 answered the first three questions correctly and then skipped the rest. The unit could have been too boring or irrelevant to this user.

It is important to realize that the data provided by the frequency table only suggests problems with the program. To find out if there really is a problem and its exact nature, it is necessary to make changes and collect more data. It is also important to interview users and find out why they responded as they did. In other words, this kind of data gives you ideas about potential problems with the program...but you then have to track down the specifics through further questioning.

The data table shown in Figure 10-2 is only one type of analysis that you can perform. Figure 10-3 shows another kind of data table that produces an item frequency matrix. This table tells you exactly what choices were made by each user for a particular question. The choices could be different response alternatives in a multiple choice question, selections from a menu, or words/phrases matched by keywords. In the latter case, it is common to provide a list of all words typed in that were not matched. This helps determine what additional keywords should be added.

PROGRAM:ATM01 UNIT: WDL02 QUES: 013

User	A1	A2	A3	A4	A5
	Response Alternatives				
U1	1				
U2			1		
U3	1				1
U4		1			
U5				1	
U6				1	
Total	2	1	1	2	1

Figure 10-3

The column totals in Figure 10-3 indicate the number of times each alternative was selected. Note that user 3 picked two alternatives (A1, A5). This suggests that A5 was a help or hint which resulted in the selection of A1. In questions where the user can make a number of selections, it is often useful to show the order of selection in the table.

Instead of (or in addition to) responses, it is also possible to record the amount of time it took a user to respond to a question, choose an option or to complete a module. The time taken to respond is called *response latency.* It is measured from the time the question, problem or option is presented until the user makes a response. Response latency is often a direct measure of how long it takes to complete an online transaction. Response latency data can also be used to make inferences about how well a user understands a concept. The faster the user responds, the better they understand the concept they were being asked about.

The type of data shown in Figures 10-2 and 10-3 provides detailed information on what users are doing as they go through a program. This kind of data should be collected during pilot testing of a program to determine what revisions are needed.

Planned Versus Haphazard Revisions

Because of the branching structure, making revisions to a program is more complicated than in a linear media such as print or video. Branching introduces a lot of interdependencies among different parts of a program. For example, data obtained at the beginning of the program may be used in later units to determine what information to present or skip. Changes to one part of a program are likely to affect other parts because of the interdependencies.

For this reason, it is important not to make revisions in a haphazard manner. When making a change to a specific sequence in a program, the flowchart corresponding to that sequence should be checked to see what other sequences will be affected and may need to be changed. A revision log should be kept that lists all changes made to a program, when they were made, who made them, and why. When problems appear as a result of changes, the revision log is very useful in tracking down what happened.

It is also important to group changes into successive versions or releases of a program rather than make the changes continuously. When a new version or release of a program is distributed, it will contain all the changes made since the previous version or release. Each new version should completely replace the previous one to prevent conflicts or confusion between the updated and current versions. In fact, instructions with the new release usually specify that the old version should be thrown away.

By releasing all new changes together, it is possible to check the interaction among changes to make sure that there are no conflicts. Sometimes two changes which work fine by themselves will not work together (because they accidentally use the same files or variables). Each version must be checked and tested as a complete program.

The frequency of new releases should be dictated by the number and significance of the changes made. During the introduction phase of a new program, it is not uncommon to distribute a new version every few months since there are typically many changes needed in the beginning. Once a program becomes mature, new versions are likely to be needed much less frequently (e.g., every six months or annually).

Collecting Attitude Data

One thing that is easy to forget when designing interactive programs is that they work better if users like them. For this reason, it is important to collect attitudinal data as well as response data during pilot testing. Table 10-4 lists examples of the type of questions that can be asked to find out if users like a program.

Table 10-4

Examples of Attitudinal Questions
1. Did you find this program easy to use? Why / Why not?
2. Did you find this program useful? Why / Why not?
3. Would you have preferred to do this acitivity without using a computer?
4. Were you ever confused while using this program? When?
5. Did you find this program too slow? Too fast? About right?
6. Was the content of the program accurate and up to date?
7. Did the program seem well organized to you? Why not?
8. Were you able to move around in the program as you wanted?
9. Were the screen displays easy to read and understand?
10. Would you recommend this program to someone else? Why / Why not?

Typically, attitudinal questions are phrased so that the user can agree or disagree on a 5 point scale. Half of the questions would be phrased positively and half negatively to avoid a question set bias. Open response questions should be included too. The user should be asked to explain what they liked and disliked about specific units or sequences.

Attitudinal information can be collected in online or offline form. Online data collection has a number of advantages over an offline format. Brief questionnaires can be inserted after each unit or specific sequences to get the user's immediate reaction. Users may be more candid when answering online than offline where a person distributes and collects the questionnaire. The most important advantage of online questionnaires is that the data can be automatically analyzed and summarized by the program, eliminating a manual data entry or calculation step.

The Importance of Good Documentation

In Chapter 3, the importance of design specifications was discussed. Documenting the program itself is also very important. The main value of program documentation is to make revision easier. Things that seem too obvious to write down when the program is written (or were written down on loose sheets of paper) tend to become obscure a few months later when a revision is needed. Furthermore, it is very common for the person who makes revisions to a program to be someone different than the person who designed or implemented the program originally.

Table 10-5 lists some of the general characteristics of a program that should be documented. Any one of these items may be important in making subsequent revisions. In addition, each unit or sequence in the program should have its own documentation that describes all files, variables, subroutines and any special programming techniques used.

Table 10-5

Program Documentation

1. Program name, version, and copyright
2. Date of program version and documentation
3. Name and address of developer/programmer
4. Purpose and intended use of program
5. Intended user audience
6. Program duration
7. Required/optional ancillary materials
8. System requirements (memory, peripherals)
9. Program limits
10. References to program design, use or validation

Almost everyone is in favor of documentation (it's like apple pie and motherhood). However, it's often not done or not done very well. To ensure that it gets done, you must insist that the program is not complete until the documentation is finished. It must be viewed as a critical development task and listed as a step to be completed in the project schedule.

In fact, documentation should be designed, developed, tested, and "debugged" just like the programs that it describes. Testing and debugging documentation is accomplished by having someone other than the original programmer try to understand and make changes to the documented program. It helps to assign responsibility for documentation to a single individual (someone other than the original programmer).

Two classic problems with documentation are that it gets out of date and it gets lost. The same solution can minimize both of these problems: put the documentation in the program itself. If the documentation is included in the program by means of comment statements, it cannot get lost and the chances are much higher that it will get updated when the program does. This makes the program bigger but program size is seldom a significant problem these days.

10/ Quality Review

Summary

This chapter has presented the following guidelines regarding quality review:

- Use a checklist to systematically review the quality of a program.
- Use response data to find flaws in the program.
- Make revisions according to a plan, not haphazardly.
- Collect attitude data as well as response data.
- Good documentation makes revision easier.

10/ Quality Review

Appendix A
Software Quality Checklist

Program: Evaluator: Date:

Terrible OK Terrific

Screen Design 1 2 3 4 5

Are screens crowded?
Are there problems due to scrolling or overlays?
Are attentional devices used sparingly?
Are windows used to organize information?
Are different type styles/sizes used effectively?
Are graphics used whenever possible?
Are headings used routinely?

User Control 1 2 3 4 5

Does the user control pace and sequencing?
Are menus used as much as possible?
Can the user customize the program?
Are multiple control options provided?
Are defaults always provided?

Response Processing 1 2 3 4 5

Are directions and questions stated clearly?
Is pointing input used whenever possible?
Is user input always acknowledged?
Is the response analysis tolerant of answer variations?
Can users easily change answers?
Is corrective feedback always provided for errors?
Are feedback messages brief and neutral in tone?

Helps 1 2 3 4 5

Are helps as specific as possible?
Are different levels of help available?
Are helps always available and easy to access?
Is help information accurate, complete, and current?

Error Handling 1 2 3 4 5

Are answers checked for being within range?
Are errors highlighted?
Do error messages identify how to correct problems?
Does the program always provide a recovery option?

TOTAL SCORE:

Appendix B
Further Information

The preceding chapters have provided a set of guidelines for the design of interactive software. However, this book does not go into depth on the topics discussed nor does it cover many related topics. The current chapter provides additional readings and references.

Programming Techniques

The development of quality software depends upon the use of good programming methods. Here are some books on programming techniques; many of these are considered classic texts on the topic.

Bentley, J. *Programming Pearls.* Addison-Welsey, Reading, MA. 1986.

Jackson, M. *Principles of Program Design.* Academic Press, NY. 1975.

Kernighan, B. & Plauger, P. *Elements of Programming Style.* McGraw-Hill, NY. 1978.

Liffick, B. *The Software Developer's Sourcebook.* Addison-Wesley, Reading, MA. 1985.

Linger, R.C., Mills, H.D., Witt, B.I. *Structured Programming Theory and Practice.* Addison-Wesley, Reading, MA. 1979.

Mack, B. & Heath, P. (Eds.) *Guide to Good Programming.* Halsted Press, NY. 1980.

Martin, J. & McClure, C. *Diagramming Techniques for Analysts and Programmers.* Prentice-Hall, Englewood Cliffs, NJ. 1985.

Van Tassel, D. *Program Style, Design, Efficiency, Debugging and Testing.* Prentice-Hall, Englewood Cliffs, NJ. 1974.

Yourdon, E. *Techniques of Program Structure and Design.* Prentice-Hall, Englewood Cliffs, NJ. 1975.

Software Development & Engineering

The following books discuss various aspects of software development including management, costing, and scheduling.

Babich, W.A. *Software Configuration Management.* Addison-Wesley, Reading, MA. 1986.

Boehm, B.W. *Software Engineering Economics.* Prentice-Hall, Englewood Cliffs, NJ. 1981.

Brooks, F. *The Mythical Man Month.* Addison-Wesley, Reading, MA. 1975.

Gilb, T. *Software Metrics.* Winthrop, Cambridge, MA. 1977.

Halstead, M.H. *Elements of Software Science.* Elsevier/North-Holland, New York. 1977.

Horowitz, E. *Practical Strategies for Developing Large Software Systems.* Addison-Wesley, Reading, MA. 1975.

Sommerville, I. *Software Engineering (2nd Ed.).* Addison-Wesley, Reading, MA. 1986.

Human Factors of Computing

Human factors engineering is concerned with the design of effective human-machine interfaces. In recent years, a lot of attention has been given to human-computer interfaces as discussed in the following books.

Badre, A. *Directions in Human-Computer Interaction.* Ablex, Norwood, NJ. 1982.

Card, S., Moran, T.P., & Newell, A. *The Psychology of Human-Computer Interaction.* Erlbaum, Hillsdale, NJ. 1983.

Galitz, W.O. *Handbook of Screen Format Design (2nd Edition).* QED Information Sciences, Wellesley, MA. 1985.

Hartson, R. *Advances in Human/Computer Interaction.* Ablex, Norwood, NJ. 1985

Heckel, P. *The Elements of Friendly Software Design.* Warner, NY. 1982.

Martin, J. *Design of Man-Computer Dialogues.* Prentice-Hall, Englewood Cliffs, NJ. 1973.

Monk, A. *Fundamentals of Human-Computer Interaction.* Academic Press, NY. 1984.

Shneiderman, B. *Software Psychology.* Winthrop, Cambridge, MA. 1980.

Smith, W. *Using Computer Color Effectively.* Taylor & Francis, London. 1987.

Thomas, J.C. & Schneider, M. *Human Factors in Computing Systems.* Ablex, Norwood, NJ. 1984.

Helps

As discussed in Chapter 8, helps represent an important form of embedded training. Here are some articles that specifically discuss help systems.

Carroll, J.M. & Carrithers, C. Training Wheels in a User Interface. *Communications of the ACM*, August 1984, p800-806.

Cohill, A.M. & Williges, R.C. Retrieval of HELP Information for Novice Users of Interactive Computer Systems. *Human Factors*, 1985, *27(3)*, p335-343.

Houghton, R.C. Online Help Systems: A Conspectus. *Communications of the ACM,* February 1984, p128-133.

Stone, D. et al. Hypertext as a Component in a Computer Based Technical Information System. *Journal of Computer Based Instruction*, Spring 1983.

Wilensky, R., Avens, Y., & Chin, D. Talking to UNIX in English: An Overview of UC. *Communications of the ACM*, June 1984, p574-593.

Graphics

Graphics represents a special aspect of designing interactive software. The following references provide introductions to this important area of program design.

Artwick, B. *Displays, Graphics, and Animation.* Prentice-Hall, Englewood Cliffs, NJ. 1985.

Foley, J.D. & van Dam, A. *Fundamentals of Interactive Computer Graphics.* Addison-Wesley, Reading, MA. 1982.

Harrington, S. *Computer Graphics: A Programming Approach.* McGraw-Hill, NY. 1983.

Harris, D. *Computer Graphics and Applications.* Chapman & Hall, NY. 1984.

Newman, W.M. & Sproull, R.F. *Principles of Interactive Computer Graphics (2nd Ed.)* . McGraw-Hill, NY. 1979.

Park, C. *Interactive Microcomputer Graphics.* Addison-Wesley, Reading, MA. 1985.

Waite, M. & Morgan, C. *Graphics Primer for the IBM PC.* Osborne/McGraw-Hill, Berkeley, CA. 1983.

Testing and Maintenance

As discussed in Chapter 10, well tested programs do not happen by accident but are the result of a systematic testing and maintenance effort. The following books discuss software testing and maintenance methodology.

Beizer, B. *Software Testing Techniques.* Van Nostrand Reinhold, NY. 1983.

Dunn, R. & Ullman, R. *Quality Assurance for Computer Software.* McGraw-Hill, NY. 1982.

Evans, M. *Productive Software Test Management.* John Wiley & Sons, New York. 1985.

Martin, J. & McClure, C. *Software Maintenance.* Prentice-Hall, Englewood Cliffs, NJ. 1983.

Myers, G. *The Art of Software Testing.* John Wiley & Sons, New York. 1979.

Smith, T. *Secrets of Software Debugging.* TAB Books, Blue Ridge Summit, PA. 1984.

Software Documentation

The following references discuss the design of software documentation.

Brockman, J.R. *Writing Better Computer Documentation: From Paper to Screens.* Wiley-Interscience, NY. 1986.

Howard, J. What Is Good Documentation? *Byte*, March 1981.

IEEE. *Guidelines for the Documentation of Software in Industrial Computer Systems.* Institute for Electrical & Electronics Engineers, Piscataway, NJ. 1985.

Jonassen, D.H. *The Technology of Text (Vols 1 & 2).*

Educational Technology Publications, Englewood Cliffs, NJ. 1982, 1985.

Katzin, E. *How To Write A Really Good User's Manual.* Van Nostrand Reinhold, NY. 1985.

Price, J. *How to Write A Computer Manual.* Benjamin/Cummins, Menlo Park, CA. 1984.

McGehee, B.M. *Writing Software User Manuals.* Writer's Digest Books, Cincinnati, OH. 1984.

Mills, C. Bergfield & Dye, K.L. Usability Testing: User Reviews. *Technical Documentation*, 1985, p40-44.

Design of Instructional Software

Instructional programs are a common form of interactive software. The following books describe the design of instructional software.

Allessi, S.M. & Trollip, S.R. *Computer-Based Instruction: Methods and Development.* Prentice-Hall, Englewood Cliffs, NJ. 1985.

Heines, J.M. *Screen Design Strategies for Computer-Assisted Instruction.* Digital Press, Bedford, MA. 1984.

Kearsley, G. *Authoring.* Addison-Wesley, Reading, MA. 1986.

Landa, R.K. *Creating Courseware: A Beginner's Guide.* Harper & Row, NY. 1984.

Walker, D.F. & Hess, R.D. *Instructional Software: Principles and Perspectives for Design and Use.* Wadsworth, Belmont, CA. 1984.

Sleeman, D. & Brown, J.S. *Intelligent Tutoring Systems.* Academic Press, NY. 1981.

Artificial Intelligence

Artificial Intelligence (AI) is concerned with the development of programs that exhibit intelligent capabilities such as inference, reasoning and understanding. AI programming techniques are necessary to develop sophisticated interactive software. The following books outline AI concepts.

Charniak, E. & McDermott, D. *Introduction to Artificial Intelligence.* Addison-Wesley, Reading, MA. 1985.

Harmon, P. & King, D. *Expert Systems: Artificial Intelligence in Business.* John Wiley & Sons, NY. 1985.

Hayes-Roth, F., Waterman, D., & Lenat, D. *Building Expert Systems.* Addison-Wesley, Reading, MA. 1983.

King, D. (Ed.) *Parsing Natural Language.* Academic Press, NY. 1983.

Reitman, W. *Artificial Intelligence Applications for Business.* Ablox, Norwood, NJ. 1984.

Waterman, D. *A Guide to Expert Systems.* Addison-Wesley, Reading, MA. 1986.

Winograd, T. *Understanding Natural Language.* Academic Press, NY. 1972.

Winston, P. *Artificial Intelligence (2nd Ed.)* Addison-Wesley, Reading, MA. 1984.

Appendix B / Further Information

Appendix C
Software Design Tools

This Appendix describes some software tools available for personal computers that can aid the design process. These programs are mentioned as examples only; no endorsement or recommendation of specific products is intended.

AutoMentor
(IBM PC/compatibles)

Software Recording Corp.
600 Fifth Ave., 4th Fl.
San Raphael, CA 94901
(415) 258-0800

AutoMentor is an authoring system designed to work like a videotape recorder: it captures screens and sequences from another prorgam as well as letting you edit screens. It is especially useful for creating demos or tutorials for application programs.

Demo
(IBM PC/compatibles)

Software Garden Inc.
Box 238
West Newton, MA 02165
(617) 332-2240

Demo is a program developed by Dan Bricklin (one of the developers of Visicalc) specifically designed for prototyping. Demo is basically a sophisticated slide- show program with a wide range of features.

Dr. Halo
(IBM PC/compatibles)

IMSI
1299 Fourth St.
San Raphael, CA 94901
(415) 641-0400

Dr. Halo is a slideshow creation program that features a "paint" type color graphics editor and uses a mouse. The iconic interface makes the program very easy to use.

EXSYS
(IBM PC/compatibles)

EXSYS Inc.
Box 75158, Cntrl Stn 14
Albuquerque, NM 87194
(505) 836-6676

EXSYS is an inexpensive expert system generator which allows up to 5000 rules on a PC/AT. It allows data to passed to applications programs and features a built-in report generator.

HyperGraphics
(IBM PC/compatibles)

Hypergraphics Corp.
100 N. Central Expwy,
Suite 1208
Richardson, TX 75080
(214) 783-9900

A sophisticated graphics authoring system that allows you to create color text/graphics screens as well as branching programs using the screens created. It is also possible to link to other applications programs using HyperGraphics. Especially well suited to creating tutorials or demonstration disks.

Monografx
(IBM PC/compatibles)

Analytics International
1365 Massachusetts Ave.
Arlington, MA 02174
(617) 641-0400

Monografx is a screen editor that lets you create character graphics that can be displayed on monochrome displays. It is useful for prototyping.

PILOT
(IBM PC/compatibles,
Apple Macintosh)

Washington Computer Svcs
3028 Silvern Lane
Bellingham, WA 98226
(206) 734-8248

PILOT is an easy to learn authoring language that allows you to quickly create interactive programs. Allows you to create different types of graphics (image, vector, sprite), windows, function keys, and many other functions. PILOT is useful for teaching the design of interactive programs and also for prototyping.

Screen Sculptor
(IBM PC/compatibles)

Software Bottling Co.
6600 L.I. Expwy
Maspeth, NY 11378
(718) 458-3700

Screen Sculptor is a screen editor and program generator. It allows you to create text and character graphic screens including variables and range checking and then automatically generates the program for the screens created in either BASIC or PASCAL. Useful for creating data entry or customer inquiry programs.

Turbo Editor Toolbox
TurboDatabase Toolbox
Turbo Graphix Toolbox
(IBM PC/compatibles)

Borland International
4585 Scotts Valley
Scotts Valley, CA 95066
(408) 438-8400

Borland International has developed a collection of software tools that work with Turbo Pascal. The Editor Toolbox provides routines to build text editors; the Database Toolbox provides searching and sorting routines, and the Graphix Toolbox provides various graphics routines. These routines can be incorporated into programs with no licensing considerations.

Videoworks
(MacIntosh)

Hayden Software
650 Suffolk St.
Lowell, MA 01854
(800) 343-1218

A program that lets you create animations with sound effects. Useful for prototyping and creating flashy demos.

Glossary

This glossary explains important concepts and terms in the design of interactive software.

Animation: Movement of a graphic across the screen. Can be used to show dynamic processes or for visual effects. Involves rapid display and erasure of a graphic with a slight change in screen location each time.

Application Software: Programs that perform some sort of application such as word processing, database retrieval, calculations (i.e., spreadsheets), graphics design, etc.

Bit-Map: A type of display in which every picture element (pixel) can be addressed. Contrasts with raster scan type display in which only complete lines can be addressed. Bit-mapped displays allow much higher resolution text and graphics.

Branching: The control of sequence in a program.

Bugs: Errors in programs that prevent them from working as intended.

Bullet-proofing: Finding all the errors in a program by means of exhaustive testing (trial and error).

Computerese: The use of technical computer terminology.

Configuration: The particular input, output, memory and processing components associated with a computer system.

Cursor: A marker that indicates the location on the screen of the next input. The marker is usually a blinking square, line, or arrow. The cursor can be moved via arrow keys or some kind of pointing device (e.g., mouse, trackball).

Data: Any information used by a program or stored on a disk.

Glossary

Debugging: The process of finding and fixing bugs in a program.

Default: An option which is automatically selected if the user does not select or provide an alternative.

Disk: The storage medium for programs and files. Is read by and written to by a disk drive. (Disks are synonomous with diskettes).

Editor: A special type of program that lets you enter and modify text, graphics, sound/speech or other functions.

Feedback: Messages generated as a result of a user response.

File: Information (data) stored on a disk and identified by a unique name for subsequent retrieval.

Flowchart: A diagram which shows the logic flow (branching) of a program.

Function Keys: Special keys provided on the keyboard which have no fixed function. Their function is defined by a program and can be changed as often as desired.

Hardware: The physical components of a computer system (e.g., monitor, disk drives, printers).

Icons: Visual symbols used to represent options or data (e.g., a symbol of a trash can represents deletion of a file).

Interactivity: A program that provides immediate response to user input or actions.

Menu: A list of options.

(Random Access) Memory (RAM): The part of the computer where programs are stored while being executed. Measured in thousands (K) of bytes. A typical memory size for current personal computers is 512K bytes.

Mouse: An input device used on some computers to move the cursor. The mouse is a small box that can be rolled on a flat surface. The movement of the cursor on the screen matches the movement of the mouse.

Networking: Multiple computers sharing the memory, storage, or peripherals (e.g., printers) of other computers. Can be either local networks (all machines directly connected via cables) or remote networks (using telecommunications).

Overlay: To display one thing on top of another, usually by adding something to the original display.

Operating System: A program which manages the computer and applications programs. Some examples are DOS, CP/M, and Unix™.

Parser: A program which translates or decodes a symbolic or natural language sequence.

Peripherals: Input, output or storage devices (hardware) such as a mouse, printer, or disk drive.

Pilot Testing: A tryout of a program with actual users. (Has nothing to do with flying airplanes).

Pixel: The smallest point that can be addressed on a display screen (abbreviation for picture element).

Pop-up/Pull-down: A window or menu that overlays the current display when it is selected from an option list. When an option is selected from the menu or when the window is closed, it disappears.

Prototype: A sample or demonstration of the actual program.

RAM (Random Access Memory): See Memory.

Resolution: The degree of detail that can be displayed on a computer screen, usually measured in pixels.

Scrolling: Moving the top lines off the top of the screen each time something new is entered at the bottom. Contrasts with paging, in which entire screens are replaced.

Sign-on: Identifying yourself to a program or system.

Software: The programs that make a computer do something.

System Manager: A program that allows you to access multiple applications programs and transfer information between them.

Subroutine: A self-contained program that can be called by the main program.

Terminal: A device with a display and keyboard like a personal computer but with no internal memory or storage. Must be used in a network.

Tiling: Automatic alignment of windows on the screen so that they do not overlap.

Transparency: A design quality that allows the user to use a program without having to learn anything about how the program works.

UNDO: A function which undoes the last action performed by the user.

Variables: Labels given to values in a program which can change.

Vector: An ordered list of numbers.

Viewports: See windows.

Windows: Defining a portion of the screen for display. Overlapping windows are displayed on top of the current display.

Index

Index

Index

Index

Index

Index